# Faith: Key to the Heart of God

*by*

## John H. Hampsch, C.M.F.
### with Clint Kelly

Claretian Tape Ministry
P.O. Box 19100
Los Angeles, CA 90019
(323) 734-1234

Library of Congress Catalog Number 84-62433

ISBN 0-9613575-1-7

Cover Photo by Mike Dunn

PRINTED IN THE UNITED STATES OF AMERICA

Each volume in the Keyhole Series presents a peek into God's treasure room at the powerful spiritual resources available to us, His children. In so doing, we become better equipped to meet the challenges of Christlike living.

Co-author Clint Kelly is a teacher, author, journalist and publisher whose articles have appeared in dozens of secular and religious periodicals as diverse as *Charisma, Family Circle* and *American History Illustrated.* Mr. Kelly lives with his wife and four children in Everett, Washington.

# Foreword

Fr. John Hampsch, a Claretian missionary priest, has for many years had a tremendous impact on the charismatic renewal in Southern California. I am sure this influence has been felt in other places, too, but in my role as director of charismatic renewal ministries in the Archdiocese of Los Angeles, I can speak only of this area. His teachings and healing services are always well attended because the people know they will hear the Word of God preached effectively and without compromise.

Fr. John has a tremendous faith that has been built up by his commitment to God's Word as revealed in the Bible. He knows the Bible well, it is so much a part of him. And through his training in psychology and his many years of ministry he knows well how to preach this Word effectively and make it truly come alive for God's people. And God does bring life through this man's preaching. Many are led to a personal faith in Jesus they never experienced before. Many come to know the healing power of the Holy Spirit.

The effectiveness of Fr. Hampsch's teaching can be seen by his tape ministry. For years his talks have been recorded and have been so popular that the outreach of his Claretian Tape Ministry is one of the largest in the Catholic Church. We feature his tapes at our annual renewal convention; their popularity never wanes.

I am excited about Fr. John Hampsch putting his tape album, "Faith: Key to the Heart of God," into book form. It will thus be available to many more people. This book on faith is solidly built on the Scriptures and touches the reader deeply as God's word. Because Fr. John is uncompromising in his faith, his teaching is very direct and hard-hitting. But that is the special gift he brings to the renewal—teaching that cannot be ignored but calls for a response.

Fr. John's faith is not based on book knowledge but on a very personal and deeply experienced relationship with Jesus Christ as Lord and Savior. The focus of this book is on the person of Jesus and it calls the reader to be open to experience personal intimacy with the Lord. Evangelists today say this is the greatest need in the Church—to bring people to a personal discovery of Jesus Christ. This book responds to that need in a very powerful way. The discussion questions at the end of each section will help people make real what is being shared.

I recommend this book to the people I minister to in the Los Angeles area. I know Fr. John's teaching on faith will lead people closer to the Lord and will prepare the way for many miracles to be performed in His name. Also, I believe it will lead many to immerse themselves more deeply in the Scriptures. And this is how the Vatican Council said God is renewing His people. I hope Fr. John will bring many more of his teachings to the written page so we might all be touched by God in this way.

Finally, it is commendable that all of the proceeds from the sale of this book will be used to help the poor of Africa.

Fr. William Adams, C.Ss.R.
Director of charismatic renewal ministries in the Archdiocese of Los Angeles
April 1, 1985
Los Angeles, California

# TABLE OF CONTENTS

*Dynamic One:*

# The Gift Of Faith

# Miracle-Limiting Faith vs Miracle-Triggering Faith

A preacher in a rural church was giving a special service because of a severe local drought. He began by saying, "You have all come here today to pray for rain. I have just one question for you: *Where are your umbrellas?*"

This depicts the way most of us pray for things. With a vague kind of hope, we say, "I hope the Lord will cure me of cancer," or "I hope the Lord will straighten out this unhappy marriage." "I hope the Lord will get my son off drugs, help me solve my financial problems and give me the job I want." Often we don't really *expect* it to happen. Without *expectant faith*, our spiritual life can be presumed to be at the kindergarten level.

While many people feel they have great faith, it is usually less than mountain-moving. Others admit their weakness in faith but still "leave their umbrellas at home."

Faith is important because, among other reasons, it is a

criterion to determine our spiritual maturity. Examine yourself about this, as Paul urges (II Corinthians 13:5). Romans 12:3 tells us to judge ourselves by the amount of faith God has given us. So, to take a spiritual inventory, ask yourself how much faith you have. Ask how many miracles you've worked. "If you believe, you can do *anything*" (Mark 9:23; 11:23). Jesus tells us to ask the Father *anything*, believing with no doubt in Jesus' name, and we'll have it, it's ours. Try meditating on John 16:23; 20:29; Mark 11:23; Matthew 11:6 regarding the degree of faith that is attainable.

There's the story of the little Irish lady who *thought* she had great faith. After all, who has greater faith than a little Irish lady who says her prayers every day? But this lady had a fault—she was jealous of her neighbor who had an apple tree in her yard. She said, "I wish I had that apple tree in my yard. The Lord said if you have faith you can move a mountain, so I guess I could move an apple tree if I just believe." She recalled Jesus' words in Mark 11:23 where He said to ask for anything, believing, with no doubt—no doubt—and you shall have it.

So the little Irish lady thought, "All I have to do is pray that the apple tree will uproot itself during my sleep and jump the fence and plant itself in my yard." She got down on her knees beside the bed and prayed, "I believe, I really believe it, Lord. With no doubt I believe that apple tree will jump the fence and plant itself in my yard. It will be *my* apple tree. When I get up in the morning, it will be there. I believe it, I believe it, I *believe* it!" Then she hopped into bed.

Awakening the next morning she jumped out of bed, ran to the window, opened the blind, and looked out, only to see that the apple tree hadn't budged at all; it was still standing there in the neighbor's yard. Dejected , the little Irish lady pouted. "I *knew* it!" she said.

Sometimes, as with the little Irish lady, our motives are warped (James 4:3). But also, as her faith was weak (as

4

her last remark revealed), so too is ours when we'd like to think it's strong. We wonder why our prayers aren't answered. We protest that we believe, but in the back of our minds we're saying it's too good to happen, isn't it? I believe I am going to be cured but, no, I couldn't be. That is what the father of the demoniac thought when the disciples attempted to heal the child who was throwing himself on the ground and into the fire (Mark 9:17 ff). The disciples couldn't succeed. They hadn't been baptized into the Spirit, as it was not yet Pentecost. So their faith showed only partial success; it worked in some cases (Luke 10:17), but not in other situations (e.g., Luke 9:40). After the disciples failed, the father brought his sick demon-possessed boy to Jesus, saying, "I begged your disciples to cast out the demon, but they couldn't do it."

Jesus chided his disciples on the weakness of their faith, wondering aloud how much longer He would have to be with them before they believed. Jesus showed a kind of exasperation because he had told them so much about faith, and yet theirs was too weak to perform the exorcism. They prayed the exorcism prayer but they didn't succeed because of lack of faith. Jesus commanded them to bring the boy to Him. When he saw Jesus, the demon convulsed the boy, throwing him to the ground, writhing and foaming at the mouth. The grief-stricken father pleaded, "Have mercy on us and do something for my boy *if you can.*"

Now that very phrase, "if you can," showed he had doubt. There was an *if* there. He didn't say, I *know* you're going to heal him as the centurion did, whom Jesus complimented for his faith (Luke 7:9). So Jesus remonstrated with the man in a very delicate way, but very firmly, showing him his lack of faith. The disciples had their lack of faith, and the father of the child, even though he came to Jesus, lacked faith, for he still didn't believe with certainty that the miracle was going to happen.

5

"Anything is possible if *you* have faith," Jesus said to him. It is not a matter of questioning God's power; that is always there. It is a matter of knowing how to *trigger* the divine power to produce the miracle. It is not a matter of saying, "The gun is loaded, will it fire?" It's, "Can you pull the trigger?" The divine power is there, but you have to pull the trigger of faith in order to release that divine power.

*Your miracle waits behind a locked door. The key to that door is expectant faith.*

There is no other way. God's spiritual laws are as inviolable as His physical ones. What would happen if I decided to defy the law of gravity and casually jump from a 20-story building? Could I rightly expect to fly or walk away unhurt? Just as a law of nature makes it impossible to step off the roof of a 20-story building without fatal consequences, so one of God's spiritual laws says, in Hebrews 11:6, "Without faith it is *impossible* to please God."

Jesus gave a very adroit answer to the worried father of the demonized boy. It was never a question of whether *He*, Jesus, could succeed. But could the father? Jesus said *you* can do anything if *you* have faith. The demoniac's father was embarrassed because he was confronted with the fact that he didn't have faith enough. He finally realized that his faith limit was an obstacle to his own prayer. Our failure comes not from God rejecting our prayers but from ourselves putting obstacles to God's desire to answer our prayers.

Jesus made the boy's father very conscious of the fact that he was weak in his faith. The man then said, "Oh I do have faith, I do believe, but help my *unbelief*—help me to believe more." He was protesting that he had some kind of faith, otherwise he would not have approached Jesus to ask for the miracle. But he saw that he needed *more* faith. He then backtracked from an intercessory petition for his child, to a petition for more faith for himself.

In effect what the man was saying was, "I believe as God you *can* do it, but it's almost too good to believe that you *will* do it." It takes a very minimal amount of faith to believe that God can do anything. If I were to ask you, "Do you believe God could cure you of all disease?", you'd say, "Yes, I believe God is almighty, and hence can do anything." "Do you believe that God *will* do it within the next five minutes?" In that case you might say, "Well, I'm not quite so sure."

Believing that God *can* do it is part of the *virtue* of faith. Believing that He *will* do it— the positive certainty—is the *gift* of faith, the charismatic gift of faith mentioned among the nine classical charisms in I Corinthians 12:8-10, and described in Hebrews 11:1.

How does one pray for something with no doubt that it is going to happen—with the positive certainty that financial problems, marriage problems, parent-child problems, health problems will be solved, and maybe within a brief time-frame? To answer that question is to put in your hands the key to the heart of God.

Jesus cast the demon out of the child because the father admitted he had a measure of faith and needed Jesus to help him have more. Apparently the Lord gave him the *added* faith— the gift to believe that it was really going to happen.

I wasn't really aware of the distinction between the virtue of faith and the gift of faith until I studied charismatic theology after receiving the Baptism in the Holy Spirit. I knew there was something wrong with my faith because I wasn't getting the miracles I wanted in my life.

I was stumbling through my life questioning how I could get what I so much desired—especially the Baptism in the Spirit, the gift of tongues, being healed and being able to convey God's healing power to help others, et cetera. I was fumbling my way through this struggle with prayer. I did not understand the dynamic of faith, or of

7

God's power released by faith. I know a lot more about it now though I still have a long way to go in faith-growth. If faith as small as a mustard seed could move a mountain, as Jesus said in Matthew 17:20, then my faith must be far smaller than a mustard seed because I haven't been able to move a mountain yet; I still have a doubt that it would move if I were to pray for that miracle (of course, other conditions would be required also, such as God's will— e.g., I John 5:14).

# Heaven's Floodgate

Yes, I still fall far short of what God wants in my faith. I am nowhere near the ideal that He proposes, but I am working to get that kind of faith. Meanwhile, the Lord has let me grow a little bit in faith to where I've seen some remarkable things. My faith grows a bit more every time I see and hear these things through the goodness of the Lord.

We learn more and more as we go through faith experiences and our faith strengthens. I have seen many miracles brought about by the prayers of God's people. It is truly staggering to see that God is really alive and good and wants to help us. It soon becomes apparent that He has a greater desire to help us than we have a desire to be helped. He wants to heal us far more than we want to be healed. We have this warped idea that God is somewhat reluctant to help us, but that if we keep tugging at His shirttail long enough, He will reluctantly say, "Okay, okay, I'll give you your healing."

God doesn't love reluctantly; He loves with a divine compulsion. His desire to manifest that love by helping us is prompted by that same divine compulsion. *We* are the ones that put obstacles between us and the miracle, not God. It's not a question of whether *He* can do it; it's whether *I* have enough faith to let Him do it. Place the blame for failure on the petitioner, not on God. It's not God's reluctance to act, but our reluctance to surrender in inescapable faith. Our faith is often too weak to trigger that power that God wants to release. He's standing there by the floodgate of His great dam full to overflowing. All we have to do is *expect* Him to open the floodgate to release His healing love and miracle power.

This charismatic gift is especially deep after the Baptism in the Spirit as with other charisms. You can have charisms before the Baptism in the Spirit but they become much deeper and more numerous after the Baptism in the Spirit, as we see in the example of the apostles. After Pentecost, there is no record of the apostles ever failing to cast out a demon, or failing to heal the sick. After Pentecost, *everyone* Peter touched, he healed (Acts 5:16). That wasn't true before Pentecost—only some that he touched were healed. After Pentecost, everyone. There was a growth in the charisms of faith and healing.

The charisms of healing, prophecy, miracle-working and so forth—all the twenty-five charisms mentioned in the New Testament— are closely tied in with the charism of faith. When Paul lists the classical charisms which he expects to be present at least in every group, if not in every person, he puts the gift of faith right next to the gift of healing and the gift of miracle-working (e.g., walking on water, multiplying food to feed the poor, changing water into wine). Miracles cannot be worked without faith, and charismatic healing cannot be accomplished without faith.

Faith is also intertwined with other charisms such as prophecy (Romans 12:6). "If you have the gift of prophecy, then prophesy to the extent that you have *faith* to believe that God is speaking through you to the assembly." So faith is needed to *exercise* that gift, but it's also needed even to fulfill the biblical command to *desire* that gift: "Seek *earnestly* all the gifts, especially the gift of prophecy" (I Corinthians 14:1). If you always wait for

9

someone else to prophesy, you're never going to receive the gift yourself. It is faith operating through another charism— prophecy. Without faith, you don't have the gift of prophecy. Without faith, neither will there be a *growth* in the gift of prophecy. The faith will determine the level of prophecy and also all the other charisms. The more you grow in faith, the more the charismatic gifts of the Spirit operate, and the more the fruit of the Spirit will manifest itself (Galatians 5:22, 23). That's why Paul says faith can be used to evaluate your spiritual growth—to find out how far advanced you are in the spiritual life (Romans 12:3).

In Acts 3 we read of the first post-Pentecostal miracle. Peter and John approached the paralyzed man lying by the temple gate. Peter said, "I command you, in the name of Jesus Christ of Nazareth, to get up and walk!" This paralyzed cripple got up, began to leap and jump and praise God. He entered the temple with them, exploding with joy at his healing miracle.

The apostles said that it was in Jesus' name that the man had been healed—it was "faith in Jesus' name *given from above*" that caused the perfect healing. Faith *given.* It's a gift.

Keep in mind that the virtue of faith is not the same as the charismatic gift of faith. Belief in heaven and hell, the immortality of the soul, the coming rapture, eternal life— these are truths you believe on the basis of revelation of the *virtue* of faith. But we're talking here of something entirely different, namely the certitude of receiving an answer to petitionary prayer; that certitude is the charismatic gift of faith.

People often think how wonderful it would be to have a deep faith; they think that all they have to do is grit their teeth and say, "I believe!"—like the little Irish lady who tried to move the apple tree. They think that somehow by strenuously "exerting" their faith that they're going to get the answer to their prayer request. That is *not* the way to do it, as I found out the hard way. You can "exert" (practice) the virtue of faith (see Dynamic Two), but don't try to "exert" the charismatic gift of faith. Fervently reciting the Creed—"I believe in God the Father Almighty, Creator of heaven and earth..."—is exerting an act of the virtue of faith. But the *gift* of faith does not consist in believing in God and the revealed truths of God—that's the virtue of faith. The charismatic gift of faith is believing that your *prayer of petition* is going to be answered. Hebrews 11:1 says that faith is the positive certainty that what you ask for, you will receive—"the substance of things hoped for..."

Teeth gritting is not the way to faith. There is no way you can crank up the gift of faith. You must simply ask for it, humbly. When the gift of faith is operating in a very detectable degree, God overwhelms you with an intuitional certitude that what is requested will be received. I John 5:13: "I have written this to you who believe (i.e., who have the *virtue* of faith) in the Son of God so that you may know you have eternal life." Two sentences further on the writer says, "If we really *know* that He is listening when we talk to Him and make our requests, then we can be *sure* He will answer (expectancy that characterizes the *gift* of faith)."

The word for "to know" in Scripture does not usually mean "head knowledge"; it means knowledge that comes by experience. When we experience this, that God is listening to us, when we experience the reality that He is about to release this power, then it happens—*it always happens!*—as it says in I John 5:15. Heaven's floodgate opens in response to that kind of faith.

## Saintly Certitude

When I think of the healings and miracles I've witnessed, I recognize that there is always some level of faith in those who are praying for or receiving a miracle. A few times in my own life I have had the experience of being suddenly overwhelmed with the expectant certitude that an "impossible" miracle or healing was going to happen in answer to my prayer. I didn't know how it was going to happen, but I just knew that it was going to happen, and it did!

Once I was driving to the airport to catch a plane to San Antonio where I was to give a retreat to 200 nuns. I had only 15 minutes to reach the plane from downtown Los Angeles by freeway, in Friday rush-hour traffic. I said, "Lord, I've got to catch that plane to San Antonio. I don't know how you're going to do it, but I'm trusting you to work a miracle to get me there on time."

The Lord then gave me a moment of certitude that He was going to do it. Now don't ask me to explain this because I don't know how it happened during the rush hour, but there were no cars on the freeway except for a very few in the slow lane! When I came to the proper turn-off ramp, there the traffic was jammed up to a dead standstill, with just enough room for me to squeeze by and get off the ramp and on the street to the airport.

I dashed to the departure gate, arriving just as the plane's door was being closed. It was opened for me, but if I'd been another ten or fifteen seconds later, I wouldn't have made it. I plopped into my seat breathing heavily, exhausted, and gasped, "God, *how* did you do that?" I still don't know how it happened, but I had the certainty that it would.

This wasn't a "hope-I-can-make-it" sort of wish (I do that a lot). That would be a prayer of urgency: "Please, please, please, Lord..." This was a prayer of expectant faith: "I *know* you're going to do it, Lord." I recognized that moment of certitude or doubt-free expectancy was, on that occasion, a God-given gift—the charismatic gift of faith, temporary, of course, in its operation as all charisms are. I wish the Lord would grace me with that charism more often!

Once after a Mass, we were praying for some people to be healed. It happened that two ladies were brought in who were dying of terminal cancer. The doctor had advised them not to stay in the hospital at exorbitant cost, but to go home to die since both had just days to live. They were brought to this meeting from their death beds, being supported by their elbows, shuffling along a few inches at a time, almost unable to move. They sat down in comfortable chairs as they could not stand or kneel for long. After the Mass, they asked for prayers for healing. Without a miraculous healing there would be no hope of survival for either of them. I wondered, surely God wouldn't work a miracle right there, would He?

I didn't want to pray alone because Jesus always sent His apostles out two-by-two to pray for the sick: the more people praying, the better. Also, I was afraid that my own faith was not strong enough by itself to bring about this type of healing. So I invited those present to stay awhile and pray over these two sick ladies (I was aware that some people selfishly stay when they want to be prayed over themselves, but don't want to pray for anyone else).

Eight or ten people stayed to pray. As we laid hands on the first patient, the woman standing next to me had the gift of faith operating at that moment. I ascertained this because she nudged me and said, "Father, watch this. You're going to see this woman healed instantly of terminal cancer, right in front of your eyes!"

I looked at her and asked, "Are you sure? You have *no* doubt?"

She replied, "*No* doubt!"

I pressed her further, "How certain are you?"

She said, "I am as certain of this miracle about to happen as I am certain of my own existence!"

Anyone who has that much certitude definitely has the charismatic gift of faith operating at that time. Not many people have that kind of certitude, a certainty equal to the certainty of one's own existence. That's deep faith!

13

I said, "I wish I had that kind of faith. I would love to see this woman healed, but I just can't bring myself to believe it will absolutely happen for sure. But if she is healed, I'll believe a miraculous event will have taken place."

Then I realized I was experiencing tentative faith similar to that of doubting Thomas (John 22:25): "*If* I see the Lord Jesus risen from the dead and put my fingers in the wounds in his hands, and my hand in the wound in his side, then I will believe He is risen from the dead."

Such is posterior faith. It comes *after* the miracle. Almost anyone can believe in a miracle after it happens. But what about the person who *causes* the miracle to happen with faith? The anterior faith that triggers the miracle is far greater than the posterior faith that comes as a result of the miracle. I had posterior faith, but the prayer warrior beside me had anterior faith—the gift of faith. Mine was not a very high level of faith, but it was all I had to work with then.

We laid hands on the first of the two sick women and prayed. After a few moments of prayer she jumped up, although she had been lethargic just moments before from her physical exhaustion. "Something like a gentle electric current came through me when you laid hands on me," she said, "and I'm free of pain for the first time in years! I'm healed, I'm healed!"

Everyone became excited and started singing praises, except me. I was cautioning the group to take it easy, to hold down their excitement. With my background in psychology, I was always suspicious of possible tricks of the human mind, having seen people throw away their crutches and a few hours later come back to pick them up again. They had experienced a hysterical reaction, an emotional response, inducing a temporary "false healing"' (caution in credulity is usually good but can at times become almost cynical; then it is simply lack of faith).

Fortunately, no one paid any attention to me. Everyone

believed it was a miracle. I was the only one doubting, or at least suspending judgment. I told the woman to go to her doctor and get a letter from him saying he had checked her out and that the metastacized cancer was totally cured. I told her to document the case also by having two other doctors verify the results. Only then would I acknowledge that there had been a miracle.

She received documentation from several doctors later that week. They were baffled, but attested to the fact that she had indeed been healed. They could not explain how she could possibly be in perfect health. Though it was not authenticated to my satisfaction until I saw the documents a week later, everyone else had been satisfied right there on the spot.

The second woman was in exactly the same dying situation. We laid hands on her and began to pray. I expected the same testament of a miracle-to-come from the woman next to me. I looked at her out of the corner of my eye and she shook her head negatively.

I asked what she meant and she whispered to me that this second woman we were now praying for was going to die soon. Our prayers would not change things, except to help her acquiesce to God's will and to have a happy death; it was her time to go to heaven and no amount of praying would change that. We prayed for her just as fervently as we did for the first cancer patient. But in less than a week, this second lady had died.

Two questions arise. First, why did God heal one woman and not the other? Walk into any religious bookstore and you'll find a plethora of books purporting to explain the "failure" of some healing prayer. McNutt has a book on healing in which there is a chapter titled "Eleven Reasons Why People Are Not Healed." When I visited Kathryn Kuhlman in the hospital just before she died, she said, "Tell me, Father, why can't God heal everyone in the auditorium through me instead of only some? Explain this to me theologically." The question is multiform, and the answer even more so.

The second question is, how did this woman know that one patient would be healed and not the other? That's a question about the operation of the charismatic gift of faith. Both questions are answered in the Bible in two adjacent sentences. I John 5:14 and 15: "We know this, that God will listen to us whenever we ask him for anything *in line with his will.*" It you ask for something outside God's Will, you're not going to get your answer. God is not going to violate His own Will. *Some* of God's Will is conditional; for instance, He may will that this person be healed of cancer *if* we pray perseveringly and with faith, et cetera. And He may will that this person *not* be healed of cancer *if* we don't pray, if we lack faith, if there is resentment (Mark 11:25), if, if, if...

There are some aspects of God's Will that are not conditional. He may *un*conditionally will that this person go to heaven right now. *No* prayer can change His unconditional Will (Psalm 119:152; Hebrews 1:12, etc.).

God's ultimate will is His glory. That is why we exist— to give glory to God. Is glory given to God if one patient is miraculously healed and the other is not? Yes. The one that was healed miraculously is now traveling around the country giving her testimony of how she was healed instantly of terminal cancer. You may have seen her on television. Her testimony causes thousands to praise God. In this, God is being glorified; therefore, His Will is being fulfilled by His glory.

The other woman who was not healed is now undoubtedly in heaven praising God with the angels and saints and giving Him glory that way, thereby fulfilling His Will. Which one is giving the greater glory to God? I don't know. But I know this: each one of those women is doing what she is supposed to do, according to God's Will.

The human perspective of this is crazy. At the next prayer meeting, we were saying how great it was that God used us to heal one woman, but that it was too bad we couldn't bring about healing to the other one. The first patient, giving her testimony, is saying, "Thank you God for healing me." The second patient, in heaven, is saying, "Thank you Lord for *not* healing me because you gave me a different healing, the ultimate healing called death." Death is the most perfect healing you could ask for—starting your eternal life. She is now saying, "I wouldn't want to go back to earth for anything. The most perfect health on earth would be, relatively speaking, torture after tasting heaven." We foolish humans are saying, "Too bad we didn't work the miracle." She's saying, "I'm glad you didn't!"

In both patients, God found His Will fulfilled. He was glorified also by our prayer for the ladies, we are all now holier because of having prayed on that occasion and our consequent added grace brings Him added glory. All of us learned much more because of that episode. Perhaps you yourself are enriched by even reading about it now, and perhaps your faith has been lifted a notch higher in reading about the healing. So God's glory is ultimately increased in many ways by that event and its consequences.

Norman Vincent Peale says God answers prayer in one of three ways: yes, no, and wait. When He says yes, you get it the way you want it. When He says no, you get it the way He wants it— ultimately something better (Romans 8:28). When he says wait, He means keep on asking. He leads us into more dependence upon Him by our persevering in prayer, like the widow importuning the judge in the parable Jesus spoke of in Luke 18.

When it's no, it will be yes in another way. No, you won't be cured of cancer, but yes, you'll get to heaven and that will be much better than being cured of cancer.

So both women are doing God's Will, they are both content, they are both thanking God for what happened. In our narrow, petty, warped attitude we demand to know, "God, why didn't you heal her?" Like petulant little

17

children, we do not understand and we demand an explanation of every mystery. "My ways are not your ways," responds the Lord, "my thoughts are not your thoughts" (Isaiah 55:8). Weak faith tends to reject a mystery and demands that it be explained. If it were, it would no longer be a mystery. But more will be revealed to a faith-filled humble person than to a worldly-wise cynical intellectual, as Jesus says (Luke 10:21).

## Expectant Waiting

In I John 4:15 we are told if we truly *know* He is listening to us when we talk to Him and make our requests, then we can be *sure* He will answer us. This answers the second question: How did the praying lady *know* ahead of time that the first patient would be healed? Every time that gift of faith is operating in one who is under that special anointing certitude, the answer to the prayer always comes. *Always!*—whether it is raising someone from the dead or curing cancer or blindness, or anything else, as long as there is not even a hint of a doubt (Mark 11:23).

God gives charismatic gifts, such as charismatic mountain-moving faith, as they are needed for the common good (I Corinthians 12:7), not just to satisfy an individual person's petty little desires. In that way the charismatic gifts are different from the "personal" gifts found in Isaiah 11:2, such as wisdom, understanding, knowledge, etc. These *personal* gifts don't deal directly with sanctification; they ultimately affect the commonweal, building the faith of the community (except for the gift of private praying in tongues, I Corinthians 14:4).

Let's look at a few aspects of this gift of faith. In John 16:23, 24, Jesus says, "At that time, you won't need to ask me for anything for you can go directly to the Father and ask Him and and He will give you what you ask for because you use my name. Heretofore you have not asked in my name, but now I tell you, ask using my name and you will receive it and your cup of joy shall overflow."

"In His name" does not mean automatically tacking on Christ's name at the end of a prayer: "through Christ our Lord." We do that to fulfill the requirement externally, but there is an *interior* finish to go with that, a much deeper one, that is to subsume to ourselves the whole personality of Christ and let *Him* perform the miracle or present our petition to the Father. It is Jesus' power coming through you to cast out the demon or heal this cancer. The Jewish concept behind the phrase "in the name of" is the vicarious presence, a kind of a real but spiritual presence of a person speaking in and through another individual, as a Secretary of State signs a treaty "in the name of" the President.

Another aspect of the gift of faith is the element of consistent expectancy—more than an optimistic hope. That expectant faith is prescribed in James 1:5 for people that want to know God's will: Should I take this job offer? Should I move to another town? Should I get a divorce? What is God's Will? Jesus says if you want to know what God wants you to do, ask Him and He will gladly tell you for He is always ready to give a bountiful supply of wisdom to all who ask of Him. He will not resent it. *But* when you ask Him, be sure that you really *expect* Him to tell you. If you don't ask with *expectant faith*, then don't expect the Lord to give you a solid answer.

Remember the case of the woman with the hemorrhage for twelve years, referred to in Luke 8? She knew if she but touched the hem of His garment, she would be healed— and she was. And Jesus felt healing power go out from Him the moment she touched His garment. Many people were touching Him that day, but only one was touching Him with *expectant faith*. The power didn't go out to the people jostling Him in the crowd. What did Jesus tell her? "Daughter, your *faith* hath healed you. Go in peace." The woman had something that others didn't have which

19

triggered God's healing power. That was expectant faith.

In Mark 11:23 and Matthew 21:21 and elsewhere we find that freedom from doubt is required for such faith. "Ask anything, believing with no doubt, and you will have it."

Personalism in prayer is another aspect of this faith. In John 14:12 Jesus says that those who believe in Him (not themselves) will work great miracles. We're not talking about having faith in your faith or faith in your prayer. This is person-oriented faith—faith in Jesus. By this faith Jesus says you will do the same miracles He has done and even greater ones (that is a page that many Christians would like to tear out of the Bible because they don't believe what Jesus says about belief).

How many people do you know who think they can work the same miracles Jesus did? Jesus told His apostles to go out like Himself and raise the dead, and they did. Peter, Paul, and down through the centuries great charismatic saints did this. St. Vincent Ferrer raised more people from the dead than Christ did. Some saints did greater miracles than Christ, just as He promised they would, by *His* power, in *His* name.

I find very few Christians who really believe Jesus' statement in John 14:12, that they will be able to do greater miracles than He. Yet they pride themselves on their faith. They might say, "I never could have sustained the grief of bereavement at my husband's death if I didn't have faith, great faith." While priding themselves on their faith, they may fail to realize how really weak their faith is (cf. Revelation 3:17).

We may think our faith is great, yet when we don't get what we ask for, we turn and blame God. "Well, I guess you don't care about me, do you, God? I've been praying all these years and nothing happens. I prayed for the cure of my alcoholic husband fifteen years and nothing has changed, so I guess you just don't live up to your word, God."

But the deficiency is on our part, not God's. God has

plenty of power to take care of any situation, but we don't have the faith to release His power. We are obstacles to our own happiness and health. To regard Him as an inconsiderate, unkind God who is somehow against us is a very childish, immature attitude. A mature response would be to ask what God has revealed about this in His Word and then to accept His challenge to exercise high-level faith, especially in the midst of trials and hardships.

We find difficulty trusting and believing in Almighty God for the big things, while we naturally trust humans in some of the most preposterous everyday situations. Example: You are traveling down a two-lane highway at 55 miles per hour. A car approaches at the same speed (combined potential impact speed of 110 miles per hour). Without a moment's thought, you take it on faith that:

1) the other driver, a perfect stranger, is properly trained, a licensed operator under complete control, not drunk, not furious with his wife, not filing for bankruptcy, with eyesight and reflexes in topnotch condition, and

2) both automobiles are in adequate mechanical shape with no chance of sudden malfunction, and tires not about to blow causing either vehicle to veer out of control.

That implies a pervasive natural faith, despite the well-publicized fact that more deaths have occurred in automobile accidents than in all the wars of this century combined! Paradoxically, our faith in fallible humans often outweighs our faith in God!

The element of calm expectancy in faith is not presumption, but childlike simplicity. A friend of mine, while filling her gas tank, was warned by the attendant that her tires were bald. "To drive in the State of California with less than a quarter inch of tread is against the law," he said. "Besides, you are endangering your own life. On a wet freeway, you might skid and kill yourself!"

She replied, "I can't afford new tires."

"Okay, it's your life, lady. If you want to drive that way, go ahead."

"All right, I can't pay for them but go ahead and put new tires on the car and the Lord will pay the bill. Send the bill to Him."

"I don't know the Lord's address," the attendant parried.

Calmly came the reply, "Well, the Lord's going to pay for them because I can't pay for them." The attendant stared back at her as if she had two heads.

But he put new tires on the car and the bill came to $115.17. The next day she received a letter from a company that she had worked for years before. The letter said they were closing the company, and in checking their files they noticed that they had neglected to give her severance pay when she had quit working there several years before. Enclosed was a check for $115.17. To the penny.

Her reaction was, "Well, of course! Ask and you shall receive."

That's expectant faith. It wasn't a matter of hoping the Lord would take care of the situation. It was rather knowing He was going to take care of it. The Lord gave her that certainty. She did not crank it up. It came as an outpouring of the Holy Spirit.

There was a lawyer I knew who wanted to move from one part of California to another. He wanted a house with Victorian architecture in a certain area of San Jose and he wanted his law offices in the house so he wouldn't have to drive to work. That meant coping with zoning laws, seeking a particular design, etc.—in short, all kinds of problems. His realtor said he had placed too many demands on the hunt, that it was an impossibility to find exactly what he wanted. The lawyer's reply was, "Don't worry. The Lord will take care of it."

Sure enough, he found exactly the house he wanted in the city he wanted in the area he wanted. It was perfect except that it was going to cost him about $3,000 to refurbish the house to put the law offices in as he required.

The lawyer didn't have the money but his wife said not to worry about it. The Lord would provide. They prayed and asked not for $3,000 but for the gift of faith to believe they would get the $3,000. The wife said after that she knew it would arrive in a few days from she knew not where.

The next day they received a letter from a long lost relative, an aunt back East some place. It read, "I don't have many living relatives. I'm getting old and I don't want the government to get all my inheritance tax. So to make sure I don't have to spend this all on inheritance tax, I'm giving away my estate now. Here is your portion." It was, of course, a check for $3,000.

Often we set confining limits on our faith, afraid to ask "too much." A friend of mine and his wife are farmers. They had a number of accidents on their tractors and things, and their insurance premiums were pretty high. They didn't want any more accidents to make their premiums go even higher. But while they were driving one day in their pickup truck, another truck in front of them kicked up a rock. It struck their windshield and, though they were not injured, the couple was faced with a crack clear across their line of vision. It was very irritating because the refraction from that crack meant they had to look over or under it.

The farmer knew if he reported the damage, up would go the insurance premiums. He decided just to let it go. Then he asked his wife if they shouldn't pray for the Lord to heal the windshield. The wife was dubious.

God heals broken bones, He heals tumors, He moves mountains. Why wouldn't He heal the windshield? They had never prayed for a mechanical healing before, but not to do so would mean placing limits on God's power. They proceeded to pray and pray and pray, but nothing happened.

They stopped for a hamburger along the roadside. After the meal, they returned to the truck and drove on. As they traveled down the road, it dawned on them that there was no longer a crack in the windshield, that it had been healed while they were in the restaurant!

It was such an extraordinary thing and they were so excited about it, they wanted to tell me about it right away. I was giving a retreat many miles away. They cancelled their plans for the whole day and drove a 400-mile round trip to where I was preaching. They asked me to get inside the cab of the truck and look at the windshield, feel it and generally check it out for problems. Nothing was wrong with that windshield inside or out.

I know those people. They are reliable, trustworthy, good people, very charismatic. How many people do you know who have faith like that? Not people who merely *claim* they have such great faith and really don't. Most people don't have enough faith to even pray for that kind of miracle, much less believe it is actually going to happen. It is kindergarten faith that most of us live in. We don't know the powers that are available to us and we don't use those powers.

## High Octane Healing

Once I was anointing with oil after teaching for healing. About 100 people were still there, most having left already. After I went a few feet past one woman I anointed, she suddenly began to scream. I ran over and asked her what was the matter. "I'm healed, I'm healed!" she shouted.

I asked her what exactly she had been healed of. "When I came in here tonight, I was blind," she replied. "And now I can see!" Her husband came running over, hugged her and cried. He was almost delirious. We all stopped what we were doing and began to sing and praise God. She had had tremendous faith, faith enough to believe that she was going to be healed of blindness. And she was.

On another occasion, I was in a hotel in San Diego following a local television appearance. It was past midnight after a charismatic conference that was being held there, and many participants were jostling to be prayed over before leaving. There was one fellow who kept getting pushed out of the way. He waited until everyone else was finished, then came up to me. I asked his need and he let me know that he had a congenital total deafness, with consequent impairment of speech. Through a genetic inheritance factor, every member of his family had no eardrums. This was a brilliant young man who could speak seven languages but could hear none of them.

He was certain he was going to be healed. As we prayed over him he heard something pop in his right ear. He was amazed for now he could hear in his right ear. We told him to check with a doctor which he did the following day. He went to his own specialist, a Jewish doctor who did not believe in Christ as a Healer or in miraculous healing. Upon examining this patient, however, he was astonished at what he saw. An eardrum had grown in the man's right ear and he could pass the hearing tests! Still deaf in the left ear, he now had perfect hearing in the right ear. With unquestioning faith, the young man invited the flabbergasted doctor to attend the charismatic conference with him the following night to watch the other ear get healed!

The doctor came, disbelieving, but with his little medical satchel with ear-examining instruments. When his patient came up on the stage, we prayed over the other ear, and it opened as well. The doctor was invited up to check the ear and test the hearing. He could not believe what he had witnessed.

I had breakfast with the healed man the next morning. I asked how he liked his new gift of hearing. He said, "This is an unbelievable experience. I often wondered what a barking dog sounded like and this morning I heard a dog bark. What an experience! And I've never been able to hear my girlfriend's voice. Today I heard her voice. I'd never used a telephone before today. I called San Francisco from San Diego and talked to my friends who were elated and couldn't believe I was using a phone. They are so excited that they are flying down this afternoon to celebrate the miracle with me!"

One ear at a time was healed—a two-phase miracle. This young man had no-doubt faith, which enabled others to see that God is alive, *really alive.* He wants to do things for us—all we have to do is release His power by exercising faith.

One of the most remarkable cases I've seen took place in Spokane, Washington. A young man about 19 years of age had been a thalidomide baby. He had no left arm but a left hand that grew out of the shoulder like a flipper. His right arm was overdeveloped, huge and muscular, making him unbalanced. A group recalling Jesus' healing of the man with the withered hand (Mark 3:5) prayed over that man for twenty minutes. That was the time it took for his left arm to grow out, inch by inch, to full normalcy while the right arm was normalized during the same prayer. A twenty-minute miracle! They're still talking about that in Spokane, a truly astonishing miracle!

Jesus healed the withered arm of the man in the temple. That same Jesus also said, "You who believe in me can do the same miracles I have done and even greater ones" (John 14:12). But how many people do you know with the faith to believe in the restoration of an arm that practically didn't exist? The Bible says that Jesus caused limbs to grow that weren't there before. You can do the same thing, He said, *if you have faith.*

During a monthly charismatic Mass, the testimonies that people presented were not too exciting—the healing of a common cold, that sort of thing, things that were not really building up the faith of the community. So the core group agreed to come a half an hour early each month and pray in the sacristy that God would really pour out His miraculous healing power to produce faith-building testimonies.

When it was time for the testimonies at the following meeting, a lady came up to the microphone and thanked everyone for praying. "I told you I was going to the hospital last week for a radical mastectomy because of cancer of the breast. I went in and had the operation. It was very successful and I want to thank you all for praying for me. The doctors are very elated and mystified because the breast was restored and grew back overnight!"

And that was only our first testimony after praying for miracles! A whole series of such testimonies came forth that night. Faith was exploding through the crowd like popcorn popping. The more miracles you witness or hear of, the more your faith grows. The exceptions are those who scorn all miracles. Such persons have anemic faith, if any at all. Some people have just enough faith to believe minor miracles but not faith to believe in major ones like healing of blindness or resuscitation from the dead. God does not actually allow people who have weak faith to see things like that (cf. Luke 10:21 and 23). I think it is God's way of controlling sensationalism in the charismatic renewal.

Once in awhile something will get publicized, as happened in *The National Enquirer*. In Blue Cloud, Minnesota, some Indians were prayed over for their rotting teeth to be healed. God healed every one of them by giving them miraculously filled teeth—every cavity filled with gold. That hit the headlines. The *Enquirer* paid to send dental experts out there to examine those Indians (I heard one of the Indian girls give a description of this on tape). One of the representatives from the American Dental Association remarked that those were the best fillings he'd ever seen!

Some friends of mine—husband and wife—showed me their own miraculously filled teeth. Most of these happenings never reach the mass media. Because there's doubt, God seems to suppress publicity about them. You'll find people who wonder why they never see any miracles. They may hear about some of these things, yet never witness them themselves. If they've never seen a miracle, it is because they have never exercised the gift of faith. Only those who have faith are the ones who are privy to the miraculous. The others just say they don't believe miracles happen because they never see them happen. They probably never will.

You, too, can have access to the miraculous. God tells you how in the Scriptures. But if you are the type of person who always demands proof—like doubting Thomas—you probably will never witness a miracle.

When I was at a retreat for priests, I hurried down to the dining room to get a quick cup of coffee. I put some powdered coffee into a Styrofoam cup, went over to the big urn marked "hot water" and filled the cup. I gulped it down fast and immediately recognized that it wasn't hot water at all, but a hot acid-like substance used to clean the inside of the urn. My throat felt on fire as I staggered to the kitchen in agony and saw the container that read "poison—fatal if swallowed."

It was torture waiting while they called the poison control center. The doctor told them to read over the phone the ingredients on the container. His reply was that I probably would not survive, but if I did, I would possibly never be able to speak. They would try to save my life, but doubted they could save my voice.

The doctor said I was too far from town for an ambulance to get there and back in time so someone at the retreat should rush me to the hospital where the emergency team would be waiting. In agonizing pain I waited for someone to bring the car around to take me to the emergency room. Then it was as if the Lord spoke to me interiorly, telling me to believe in His Word. When you're dying, it's easier to have great faith! So I told the Lord I believed in His Word, specifically Mark 16:18: "Those who believe in me, even though they drink poison, it will do them no harm."

I claimed that biblical promise, and in less than one minute I was perfectly normal! I guess they're still waiting for me in that emergency room!

## Becoming Faith-Fit

Fine, you say. So how do I get the gift of faith?·You cannot create a sense of "no doubt." You cannot create within yourself the absolute certainty the mountain is going to move. But God can *give* you the certainty *if you pray for it.* Those who are Baptized in the Spirit have a much better chance of receiving this certainty of faith than those who aren't because it is a charismatic gift (I Corinthians 12:8). Remember:

1. To receive the gift of faith, you must practice the virtue of faith (see Dynamic Two). Believe in Jesus and in all truths that He has revealed, and reaffirm your faith in that revelation.

2. Seek the gift earnestly. Paul commands this. In I Corinthians 14:1 he says to seek *earnestly* all the charismatic gifts. You won't get *all* the charismatic gifts, especially ministerial gifts. But you should *seek* them all, including the gift of faith. Have you asked for it *earnestly?* If your child were dying, you would pray earnestly. In a crisis you pray earnestly ("No atheist in a foxhole"). But what about praying earnestly for things that aren't that dramatic, like the gift of the discernment of spirits, or prophecy, or faith? You give far more glory to God by having the faith than by having healing resulting from that faith. But do you pray for that faith as earnestly as you pray for the healing?

3. If you want the gift of faith, use the gift of praying in tongues. Paul says this indirectly in Romans 8:26 and 27: "By our *faith*, the Holy Spirit helps us with our daily problems and in our *praying.*" Problems and prayer. How does He help? In faith. Where does the faith come in? He explains it by saying, "We don't know how we should pray

or what we should pray for. The Holy Spirit will pray within us with such feeling that it cannot be expressed in words."

The groaning in the Spirit—that's the gift of tongues used even by Jesus (Hebrews 5:7). "The Father who understands what the Spirit is saying within your heart will answer in accordance with His Will" (Romans 8:27). Gaining the gift of faith will be enhanced through praying in tongues, which both Paul and Jesus say we should *all* have (I Corinthians 14:5 and Mark 16:17).

I Corinthians 14:23 warns that those who do not have the charismatic gifts will think that those are crazy who speak in tongues. Expect this persecution because they don't appreciate this gift who don't have it. In their ignorance they say it is either foolish or beyond their attaining. They won't even ask for it, though the Bible commands them to ask for it. That is typical of the prejudice we meet in fostering the charismatic renewal.

The three means of cultivating the *gift* of faith are: by practicing the *virtue* of faith, by "earnestly seeking" the gift of faith and by praying in tongues. We all have some level of faith; that's where God starts—He takes us where we are. As Isaiah said, God will not crush the bruised reed or quench the smouldering flax (Isaiah 42:3). But whatever faith you have, don't lose it. In Hebrews 10:38 we are warned not to slip back in our faith, for that is not pleasing to God.

Without faith, you cannot please God (Hebrews 11:6). The more faith you have, the more you please God. And the more you please God, the more He'll please you by filling your needs.

# Taking a Second Look
## at the Gift of Faith

**Ask Yourself (Or discuss with a study group)...**

1. What is the gift of faith?

2. Why was Jesus exasperated with His apostles in the case of the demoniac child?

3. How does Hebrews 11:6 apply to the gift of faith?

4. How do we learn through faith?

5. How does Baptism in the Spirit enhance the gift of faith?

6. How are the other gifts of the Spirit tied into the gift of faith?

7. What is the difference between the virtue and the gift of faith?

8. Why is posterior faith the weakest kind?

9. Why was one cancerous woman healed and the other not, since both had faith?

10. Why is expectant faith the strongest kind?

11. In what ways are we obstacles to our own happiness and health?

12. What are the essential differences between natural faith and spiritual faith?

13. What three things must we do to receive the gift of faith?

*Dynamic Two:*

# The Virtue Of Faith

There was a preacher in a small Ozark village, the only preacher in town, who decided in his zeal that he had a serious obligation to make sure everyone was baptized. A rather high-pressure type of person, he decided with the help of some strong men to make sure everyone was immersed in the river.

He told each person in this small town to gather at the river Sunday morning for baptism. One lady was rather resistant to this idea of high-pressure religion but in spite of all her kicking and struggling, the strong men were able to edge her into the river. The minister dunked her under the water and when she came up, he asked, "Do you believe?" She said, "No!" So he dunked her under again and held her there for a very long time thinking baptism might take effect the longer he kept her under.

Up she came again at last, gasping for air, and the minister asked again, "Do you believe now?" She said, "No!" So he pushed her under a third time and held her so long she almost drowned. At last she came up gulping for air and the minister thundered, "Now do you believe?" and she said, "Yes!"

The preacher asked, "*What* do you believe?" She said, "I believe you're trying to drown me, you darn fool!"

With baptism we associate belief. We recall Jesus saying in Mark 16:16, "He who believes and is baptized will be saved." Then He says, not he who doesn't believe, but he who *refuses* to believe will be damned. A baby doesn't believe but neither does a baby refuse to believe.

The positive belief, for those who are capable of that belief, along with baptism, is the initial act by which we become Christians. There is a very close association between belief and baptism. We find this in Acts 2:41: "Those who *believed* and were *baptized* that day totaled 3,000." That was the post-Pentecostal explosion of converts. Or Acts 18:8 in Corinth when Cripus, who was the leader of the synagogue, *believed* in the Lord and was *baptized.*

Wherever in Scripture it speaks of baptizing anyone, it is always associated with the idea of belief, the basic act of faith. In Acts 8:36 and 37 we read of the eunuch being converted by Philip who was miraculously transported there. The eunuch asked, after Philip has explained the passages from Isaiah referring to Christ, if there was any reason why he couldn't be baptized right then and there. Philip asked if he *believed*, and he answered yes. The baptism that followed was coupled with the initial belief, as it always is in Scripture.

St. Thomas Aquinas in the 13th Century wanted to investigate the practice of infant baptism which had been frequently practiced from the 11th Century. Adult baptism was the only type of baptism, outside of emergencies, to be had in the early church. In the 11th Century when the church formed the sacramental system, infant baptism became a more extensively accepted custom. St. Thomas Aquinas asked the question, is infant baptism valid? An infant could not make an act of faith. It could not practice faith, or for that matter any of the 56 virtues listed in the catalog of virtues.

He concluded that infant baptism was valid but not fruitful until such time as a child was old enough, with the help of parents or godparents, to make a committed act of faith in Jesus as Savior. So the act of faith would come probably seven or eight years at least after the infant baptism. It completes the baptism. The faith and the baptism must go together, if not simultaneously, at least sequentially.

That has a lot to do with our initiation into Christianity, but that's only the first operation of faith. Then we must personalize that completing act of baptism by saying, "I accept Jesus as my *personal* Savior. He died for me as if I were the only one that ever existed." That is the born again experience, a completion of the sacramental baptism. St. Paul articulates this in Galatians 2:20: "The Lord has loved *me*, and delivered himself for *me*."

## Operational Christianity

In John 1:12 we read: "As many as received him, he gave them power to become the children of God." Receiving or appropriating salvation to oneself requires acknowledging not only that Jesus is *the* Savior, but that He is *my* Savior. In the words of St. Augustine, "He loved each of us as if there were only one of us." Until we grasp that kind of redemptive love, we're not born again. Once we do, we are "faith-disposed" to make a personal commitment to Christ as Lord and Savior. By being sorry for our sins and asking the Lord's forgiveness we become eligible to receive the benefits of redemption and we are placed securely on the path to heaven.

That is the initial act that unfortunately many Christians never complete. For that matter, the vast majority of Christians in the world's 22,800 Christian denominations are not born again Christians. Certainly far less than 50 percent of Christians are born again Christians. That is a tragedy because it means that they haven't moved into what we might call *operational* Christianity. Pope Paul VI decried this fact in his apostolic letter on evangelization in the seventies. He said that unfortunately most Christians are sacramentalized (baptism, matrimony, eucharist, etc.) but are not evangelized. They have not received the basic gospel message, the full effect of the completed baptism. He said we shouldn't try to evangelize the world and make converts and persuade people to come into the Kingdom of God if we ourselves aren't deep into the Kingdom.

So we have to get back to the personal commitment to Christ where we not only *know about* Jesus but we *know* Jesus. You can know about Him by reading the Bible, listening to sermons, studying the historical facts of His life, but that is all theological knowledge of limited spiritual value. If knowledge about Jesus, about God, was sanctifying, then every theologian would be a saint since they know more about God academically than anyone else. But being a theologian does not make one a saint. It is not knowing about Him, it is knowing Him, that interpersonal relationship, that one-to-one closeness—the feel of His personality, the feel of His friendship, that intimacy that comes from faith and is developed through continued faith. That is the first level of that faith.

Obviously we're talking of person-oriented faith, part of the virtue of faith. The charismatic *gift* of faith, as we have explained, deals only with expecting an answer to prayer, solving life's problems. The *virtue* of faith is directed primarily to God. Belief in a person in the context of a personal relationship. Belief in Jesus as *my* Lord and Savior. "He is my Savior, my Redeemer, my rock of salvation, my shield..." (Psalm 144:2). Not *our*, not *the*, but *my*. Personal.

This concept is overlooked in a great deal of Christian preaching and practice. Most people don't relate to the Lord Jesus in a personal way. For them, it is not cultivated as a friendship relationship. It is an historical relationship. Jesus is regarded simply as an historical figure who set up a system of ethical and religious norms 2,000 years ago. There is no acknowledgment of a personal relationship with Him.

The key element about the virtue of faith is that it starts with a focus on a person. Then it spills over secondarily into what the person says or reveals—revelation of truths or doctrines.

When Pope John XXIII opened the Second Vatican Council in the sixties, he said there was something missing in the Church's catechetical system, especially in terms of how we receive God's revelation. It is characterized by the concept of faith. It had been formerly defined as believing in all the truths God has revealed directly through the Church. That's not wrong, it's just incomplete. And there is a wrong emphasis in that definition.

A commission was established that wrote a document called the Decree on Revelation. It took them four years to write one sentence. The sentence was revised five times before it was deemed acceptable. It said, in effect, that there are two aspects to the virtue of faith: a *primary faith* that is a belief in a Person, God, as the Revealer of truth. The one through whom He reveals directly is Jesus ("No man comes unto the Father but by me..."), and a *secondary faith* that focuses one's belief on what that Person has said or revealed—namely teachings, doctrine. For years the secondary faith had been emphasized while the primary faith was less emphasized.

We never neglected primary faith. We've always believed in Jesus, but when it came to the practice of faith, we tried to exert secondary faith in our practice of the virtue. Now the emphasis is where it belongs: we must believe in Jesus. He is the One. We must believe in God who is epitomized in the contactable figure of the divine-human being, Jesus—the contact point between man and God.

# Loving The Revealer

The secondary faith is what Jesus revealed. We believe in these things because we believe in the Revealer. We have faith in the resurrection of Christ, the Trinity, the immortality of the soul (and secondary faith teachings) because of our primary faith in Christ. But we adhere to these teachings *in proportion* to our adherence to primary faith.

An example by analogy may clarify this. A man calls his wife from work and says, "Honey, I'm going to be late coming home from work tonight. I have to work until midnight at the office, so don't prepare supper for me." Now she's a good wife and he's a good husband and they have a good marriage. He has proven himself to be very trustworthy and she has the greatest confidence in him. She does not doubt for a moment that what he says is true. She does not think he is going to be running around with his secretary at the local bar or motel. She believes in *what he says* because she believes in *him*. She believes in the revealed statement because she believes in the revealer. To the extent that she believes in him, to that extent she believes in what he says.

The parallel is obvious. To the extent that we believe in Jesus (and there are many degrees of that), we believe and adhere to what He tells us.

You really can't have one without the other. If you see how closely they are related, then you have a measuring stick by which to determine how deep your own faith is. You are thereby able to apply what Paul says in Romans 12:3: "Judge yourself by the amount of faith God has given you." We can take a spiritual inventory, as we did with the *gift* of faith; we can judge ourselves on how much of the *virtue* of faith we have (cf II Corinthians 13:5).

A faith inventory will enable us to calibrate our spiritual maturity. If we end up disappointed by this investigation, let it spur us to move higher. Don't become discouraged. You may find you are a mess. Ask the Lord to bless the mess you are, but do not allow it to immobilize you. Allow it instead to refine you in your faith.

In John 5:39, Jesus tells the scribes and Pharisees, "You search the scriptures"—the Word of God, the content of secondary faith—"because you believe they will give you eternal life, but those very scriptures point to Me"—the content of primary faith. There are over a thousand prophecies in the Old Testament that point to Christ as the Messiah. The Word of God gives you eternal life only because the Incarnate Word gives you eternal life (I Thessalonians 2:13). The scribes and Pharisees emphasized secondary faith while de-emphasizing primary faith. They had found the doctrine target, but not the *person* target, of their faith.

In John 8:47, Jesus says, "Anyone whose father is God listens gladly to the words of God, and since you don't, it proves you aren't his children." Hence, accepting the Revealer implies accepting the revealed truth He presents. Primary and secondary faith constitute a "package deal."

The doctrine of the Eucharist shows how this is done. According to Cardinal Newman, in the last century there have been 157 interpretations of the words, "This is my body." Of those, 90 interpretations are currently in use by different Christian denominations. Four times in John 6 Jesus gives the promise of the rapture for those who partake of the Eucharist. "He who eats my flesh and drinks my blood, I will raise him up on the last day; he who does not eat my flesh and drink my blood will not have life in him." I Corinthians 11:29 tells us that anyone who eats the bread and drinks the wine not discerning therein the body and blood of the Lord is guilty of the death of the Lord. That makes it very real, very sacred.

After stressing the importance of this doctrine in John 6, Jesus went on to say we must eat His flesh and drink His blood. It sounded like cannibalism! The Jews were

41

turned off by it. His very disciples, who had believed Him, watched the miracles and just been involved in an audience-participation miracle (eating the multiplied bread), said, "That's a hard saying. Who can take it?" and walked away. Jesus did not call them back and try to explain it away. He just turned to his apostles and asked, "Will you also go away?" He was not going to change His doctrine. If He had to lose them, He would. He was not going to compromise the truth He was revealing.

Peter, speaking up for the apostles as usual, said, "Lord, to whom shall we go? *You* alone have the *words* of eternal life." They had primary faith in Him, therefore they had to have secondary faith in what He was saying. Peter did not understand the doctrine of the Eucharist. But he accepted the doctrine because he accepted Christ; accepting the Revealer, he accepted the truth revealed by that Revealer. If it was explained *how* it could be done, it would not be faith, it would be knowledge, science. Faith transcends science.

Faith is believing without evidence but relying on the validity of the testimony of someone who is reliable. It is person-based, not evidence-based.

The intensity of adherence to doctrine flows from the intensity of adherence to the revealer who reveals the doctrine. We can reverse the process and ask how strongly we believe a truth that is revealed; that will tell us how much faith we have in Jesus, the Revealer. It will tell us the level of our personal commitment.

Another example is found in John 11 when Jesus came to raise Lazarus from the dead. Martha went out to meet Him and said, "Lord, if you had been here, my brother Lazarus would not have died." So Jesus then challenged her to secondary belief. "Don't you believe in the resurrection of the body (the rapture)?" He asked her. She replied, "Yes, Lord, I believe that you are the Messiah, the son of God." Again the connection is established between secondary and primary faith. She believed in the truth of

42

the resurrection because she believed in Jesus the Messiah, the Revealer.

In John 5:24, Jesus says, "Anyone who listens to my message"—secondary faith—"believes in God who sent me"— primary faith.

## Steak And Potatoes Faith

There are atheists who believe that Jesus died on the cross. There are pagans who might believe Jesus actually died as a martyr to save the world, but it doesn't necessarily mean they accept it. For that matter, there are so-called Christians who believe that Jesus died to save mankind but they have not accepted that fact personally. I John 5:1 says that if you believe that Jesus is the Christ, that He is God's Son and the Savior, then you are a child of God.

Hebrews 10:39 says our faith in Him (primary faith) assures our salvation. I Corinthians 15:1-3, I John 5:13 and many other Scriptures affirm the same thing. That is the basic level.

You may say you've done that. You've watched Christian television and prayed the sinner's prayer ("All you people out there in television land get down on your knees now and take Jesus for your personal Savior"). You've done that, perhaps many times. That's beautiful, and it's good to have it renewed. The problem, however, is this: a person who makes that act of faith often thinks that is all there is to faith—getting saved. "Saved" is a relative term because Paul in Ephesians 4:30 implies a second level of salvation. He says, in effect, that our salvation is not completed here, it is completed when we get to heaven. And again in Philippians 2:12 he says to work out one's salvation in fear and trembling, implying that we have not fully arrived yet. We have security because Jesus said, "Those the Father has given me, no one will snatch from my hands." And I John 3:9 says no one who has become part of God's family makes a practice of sinning because Christ, God's Son, holds him securely—"saved—"and the devil cannot get his hands on him. Such a one is saved in the sense that he is locked into a path to heaven, and that's beautiful.

But to think that is all there is to faith is to cultivate what I call kindergarten spirituality.

Hebrews 6:1 says not to stop there. "Stop going over the same old ground again and again, always teaching those first lessons about Christ. But let us go on instead to the other things and become mature in our understanding as *strong Christians ought to be.*" Let's stop eating the baby pablum of Christian spirituality, as important as that is to get started. Let's move on to something more sublime, more advanced.

In Colossians 2:6 Paul says, just as you believed in the Lord to save you, now believe Him also to solve each day's problems. This moves us to a different level, that of "problematic" faith. Trust Him not just for the big problems like getting cured of cancer or digging out from under financial ruin, but little things too, like finding a parking slot at the shopping mall or being cured of dandruff. Romans 8:26 promises the Holy Spirit will help us with our prayer and our daily *problems.*

This problematic faith is second stage faith—that which goes beyond. It means living by faith as urged by Galatians 3:11. Not just the faith that completes baptism, but everyday living that is *filled* with faith throughout every facet of life, especially in life's problems.

The third stage of faith development goes beyond knowing that God can and will solve problems. The third stage I call "yielding" faith, belief in and consequent surrender to God's love for you—not in an abstract way, but in a very personal way. The child that attends religion class and recites "Jesus loves me, this I know, for the Bible tells me so" is simply making a theological statement of a truth, but that is worlds away from experiencing such love. The Pope told us in Rome at the charismatic conference in 1975 that charismatics have something that can never be learned by any kind of religious instruction, catechism class or preaching. We have, in fact, something that no Christian education could ever give us. What is it? A release of the Holy Spirit where the rosebud of His presence from baptism becomes the rose bloom of His presence by power (Acts 1:8). The primary effect of the Baptism in the Spirit, said the Pope, is the *experience* of the divine hug. Paul defines it in Ephesians 3:18 and 19: "May you *experience* for yourself how deep, how wide, how high His love really is." This stage of spirituality is characterized by a faith "so real" that you *experience* God's loving presence and are frequently aware of His "love whispers."

It manifests in a series of minor miracles, extraordinary "coincidences" and it happens 10, 20, 30, 40 times a day. You sense that God must *really* love you for it seems He is starting to respond more attentively to your needs. It's as if He is saying, "See? I do love you and these are ways in which I whisper my love for you." Finding just the right doctor with just the right medication for your problem, green lights synchronized in your favor, receiving a tax rebate just in time to buy a sale item, an encouraging phone call received at precisely the needed moment—little things that start to happen again and again and again with amazing frequency and consistency.

The experience of this love becomes very, very meaningful, especially in a contemplative kind of prayer. In Colossians 2:2 Paul wishes for us to experience Christ, to *know* Him rather than to *know about* Him. This implies a clear understanding, not just wondering how Jesus looked, how He acted, what He would say in this case—it's none of that. It is the Living Christ coming right into your life and experiencing His love, as He reveals Himself to you (John 14:21-23). Your surrender to this loving presence is the yielding faith.

45

Now, how do you believe in this love? Listen to St. John in his first epistle, chapter four, verse 16: "We know how much God loved us because we have felt his love and because *we believe him when he tells us he loves us dearly.*"

Belief in God's love, the third level of faith. And that's the real test of maturity. Tie that in with what Paul says in Romans 5:5 after saying that we should rejoice in problems that lead to patience and more trust in God, our hope and faith becoming strong and steady. When that happens "...we can hold our head high no matter what happens and know that all is well for *we know how dearly God loves us and we feel this warm love everywhere within us* because God has given us his Holy Spirit of love to fill our hearts with his love." Not with love, with *His* love. Jesus didn't say "abide in love," He said "abide in *my love*" (John 15:9 and 10). Doing this, our prayers will be answered (v. 7). Hence the apparent "phenomenon of coincidence" mentioned above.

This faith can become so intense it gives us an experience of the envelopment of that divine hug. Immediately you can perceive that this is a spiritual, not theological, response. It gives a depth to your prayer life and a kind of power over the heart of God.

Notice that all three levels of faith—the salvific, the problematic and yielding—have a common denominator, namely that they are person-oriented. They express belief in the Revealer and only incidentally in the revealed. If you believe in the revealed truth that God loves you, that's one thing. If you believe in a Lover who reveals His love, that's another. Faith relates us to the tremendous lover that is Jesus.

# Meausuring Maturity

How person-oriented is your faith? How much of this affinity do you have for God? We can measure how much the wife believes in the husband by how much she believes in what he says. Take any of the truths that God has revealed. How much do you believe in them? That will measure how much you believe in the God who revealed them (through Jesus).

How about heaven and hell? If you could really see hell in all its horror with the eyes of your face and not the eyes of your faith, you wouldn't go anywhere near sin for the rest of your life. Hell is mentioned 57 times in the Bible; we know the reality of it, but do we have to see it to believe it? How much do you believe in hell? What chances do you take with your salvation? That will tell you something about how much you believe what God has revealed.

Heaven, hell; the sheep, the goats; the right, the left; the split. In Matthew 25, Jesus says that if you do not feed the hungry, clothe the naked, visit the invalid, then "Depart from me ye cursed into the everlasting flames of hell..." If we neglect to do it to one of the least of these, we neglect to do it unto Him. We say we believe all that, but what do we do in terms of *living* that belief? Do I believe it? Do I *really* believe it? Do I *act* as if I believe it? These three questions in sequence of intensity can be asked about any revealed truth (doctrine).

Let's look at heaven, a more positive focus. In Colossians 1:5 we have a statement of secondary faith: "You are looking forward to the joys of heaven and you have been ever since the gospel was first preached to you." In Colossians 3:1-4 Paul says "since you've become alive again—been born again—now set your sights on the rich treasures and joys of heaven where He sits beside God in the place of honor and power. Let heaven fill your thoughts, let your conversation be in heaven. Don't spend your time worrying about things down here." That last sentence alone, from Scripture, could really transform our lives!

Now listen to the next sentence. "You should have as little desire for this world as a dead person has. Your real life is in heaven with Christ and God. When Christ, who is our real life, comes back to earth, you will shine with him and share in all his glories."

What does money mean to a dead millionaire? There are no pockets in a shroud. He looks back on all that money and it's like ashes. I don't care where he is on the other side of eternity, that money is useless to him. People may be fighting for it here and now but in his mind and for the rest of eternity that money is trash. And most of the things it buys are trash unless he used it to help the poor, feed the hungry. As a tool, as a means for helping people and to sustain life on earth for himself, it had worth. Paul says don't worry about things down here, and have as little desire for the things of the world as a dead person does. That statement carries a secondary faith content.

Do we do that in our lives? Paul says that anyone who clings to this life as if it were the only thing that matters is a person that needs to be pitied (I Corinthians 15:19). The worldly person is really a twisted and warped individual. But how easy it is to become worldly! We wouldn't think of giving up that favorite television program. We must have that new car. It is very easy to get caught up in materialism to the point where we become *ungenerous* with the missions, the poor, the starving. It doesn't make much impression on some that there are 40,000 people dying of starvation every day, as long as they get their three square meals a day. It is frightfully easy to lose perspective through materialism. Thus, if we have a weak secondary faith in the revealed Word of God about worldliness, it would reflect a weak primary faith in the God who revealed it.

In II Corinthians 9 Paul says the Lord will give you much so that you can give away much. He does not give you much to hoard. We are stewards, not owners.

That is just one of the thousands of things God has revealed through His Word. You've heard it, you know it, but *do you believe it*? How's your secondary faith? It is in proportion to your primary faith. If you really believe in Him, then that truth under the inspiration of the Holy Spirit will grip you and change your whole behavior. If you really love God, you can't be a materialist. You wouldn't worry about paying your bills, you'd trust the Lord to provide. You would not be concerned about what you would eat or what you would wear, only heathens and publicans do that, Jesus said (Matthew 6:31 and 32). Six times Jesus forbids us to worry about material things in Matthew 6. Jesus says, "Your heavenly Father knows you have need of these things." The worldling says, "I have to fend for myself."

On a preaching assignment in Las Vegas recently, I saw, even in the airport, slot machines with people avariciously pulling at the "one-armed bandits," plugging in their money. We stopped for a hamburger on the way from the airport and my host said to me—in contrast to what I had just seen—"I wish I didn't have to have money. I wish I could give it all away. I'm tired of fighting this worry of how to pay taxes and how to pay the bills. If I could just be free. I envy you, Father, for your freedom. You've taken a vow of poverty, you don't worry about these things. You give to the Community and they give you back what you need. No worry." He threw his money on the counter to pay for the burgers as if to say, "Thank God I got rid of some more filthy lucre!"

His desire was to become disengaged from the things of the world. Isn't it crazy, all this grabbing for money? In Las Vegas, many people are intoxicated with money-hunger, waiting for that jackpot. People who watch game shows by the hour gush, "Ooh, they won a new refrigerator; ooh, they won a new car, ooooooh..."

Authentic Christians realize that they are only stewards of God's treasures. That is one effect of secondary faith. They are not materialists in the grip of money. They are Christians in the secure grip of God's love! Hence their primary faith is reflected in this and every other form of secondary faith.

Let's try this little experiment for a moment. Imagine yourself walking out the door of a supermarket when someone comes along behind you and you hold the door for that person as an act of courtesy. Suddenly that person disappears and Jesus is standing there instead. How would you feel? What a privilege to hold the door open for Him! And yet He said as you have done it unto one of the least of these, you *have* done it unto Him (Matthew 25:40)! Why do we have to have an apparition of Jesus to realize what a privilege it is to help another human being?

Here's a housewife who cooks a meal, slaps it on a plate and shoves it in front of her husband and says, "There!" Her attitude is, "I've done what I have to do. I've cooked you a meal. I'm supposed to cook, so I did it." Suddenly the husband disappears and Jesus is there. It's a little different situation then, isn't it? Later on she's washing the dishes and realizes Jesus is coming to the next meal and is going to eat off that plate in her hands. What a difference that is going to make in the way she washes the dishes! The ordinary, prosaic, pedestrian activities of everyday life come alive when our secondary faith is alive, believing, "You have done it unto me."

At a supermarket counter, you allow someone with a smaller purchase to get ahead of you in line as an act of courtesy. Suppose that person turned out to be an angel in disguise? In Hebrews 13:2 it says to be kind to strangers, for many without knowing it have entertained angels. There are many angels in human disguise as strangers all around us all the time. Secondary faith in God's Word enables us to believe that we might be dealing with someone from another world in our everyday activities. Our secondary faith in this truth, in itself, should make us more respectful to strangers.

Do you believe you have a guardian angel? Read Psalm 91:11, Psalm 34:7 or the words of Jesus in Matthew 18:10. If you really believe in your guardian angel, you know you

50

always have a companion. Would you ever commit a sin if you could see your guardian angel? Would you ever feel lonely if you could see your guardian angel? The loneliest widow in the world would not be lonely if she truly believed in her guardian angel, not to mention the Emmanuel concept of God ("I am with you always, even to the end of the world"). Loneliness would be impossible if we really lived even one aspect of secondary faith.

But it's usually not realized, not experienced. For most Christians, secondary faith is weak because our primary faith is proportionally weak. We don't actually believe in the truths God has revealed, except in the most remote, abstract way. Correlatively, we don't believe in God and His love for us, except in the most remote, abstract way. Again, it is a matter of degree, not a matter of either-or.

Do you believe Jesus' statement that you can't have your sins forgiven if you harbor resentment? Or that that resentment will prevent you from working miracles or getting your prayers answered? Mark 11:23 implies that every Christian should be a miracle worker! Jesus said ask for anything, believing with no doubt, and it's yours. Read the next sentence (v. 25): "But before you ask for these things be sure that you forgive your brethren from your heart (a Hebrewism that means *with the totality of your being*), so that your Heavenly Father will forgive your sins." Forgive not, and you will not be forgiven (Matthew 6:15). If you harbor any resentment against anyone, living or dead, then you are not authentically Christian. You're also living in sin—not just the sin of resentment, but in the accumulated and consequently unforgiven sins as well. There are thirteen places in Scripture where it says you will not be forgiven unless you first forgive. Do you believe that? This is only one small part of the revealed Word of God. Accepting it is one small part of your secondary faith.

Should you harbor resentment against anyone—the rapist who raped you, the burglar who raided your house or the thief who stole your car, the person who broke up your marriage—it means you don't love your enemies and you are not fully Christian (John 13:35). You have to love that rapist who raped you; you don't have to *like* him (an emotional attraction), but you do have to *love* him with a benevolential love. That means you must *want good for him*. Jesus says in Luke 6:28 that you must pray for your enemies; that's benevolential love. I Peter 3:9 says, "Call down God's blessings on those who offend you." Ask God to make that criminal happy, prosperous and especially repentant. Pray for those who have injured you. If you don't, you can't call yourself a true Christian, because you are not following the basic mandate of Christianity which is love. Jesus' mandate goes beyond Old Testament requirements to love your neighbor (Leviticus 19:18); we are now required to love our enemies (Luke 6:27)—He said He did not come to destroy Old Testament morality but to improve upon it, fulfill it. If you are living only by *what was* instead of also *what is*, you cannot call yourself a Christian. Check your secondary faith.

Do you believe in human dignity? Psalm 8:5 says we are a little less than the angels. What tremendous dignity! What is your reaction to a bum on the street, a drunk on skid row, unshaven, unkempt, wallowing in his own vomit? Do you experience only revulsion? Or do you say, "There's a suffering Christ?" Do you hate the sin but not the sinner (Jude 23)? Do you see that person as a diamond in the mud? A diamond is no less precious because it is in the mud. There is a person made in the image and likeness of God paid for by the blood of Jesus, loved by God *infinitely*. If I walk by, muttering "What scum!", something's wrong with my faith; it isn't the faith that works through charity. I haven't seen by faith the full reality there. If I put on the mind of Christ (Philippians 2:5), then I see the person the way Christ does, with a heart bleeding with compassion for each suffering human. Our appreciation of human dignity, especially in the poor, the sick, the lowly, reflects our secondary faith in the revealed mandate, and through that, our primary faith is measured.

If you believe in God, then you must believe in His revealed truth. Do you believe in the reality of demonic influence? Ephesians 6 reminds us that we are not fighting against mere flesh and blood, but against principalities and powers of darkness. Do you believe that you might be contaminated with a spirit of doubt, a spirit of divorce, a spirit of selfishness, a spirit of addiction? Are you prepared to admit that you might be contaminated with the forces of evil? All Christians are at one time or another under the influence of the devil; even Jesus was, in terms of temptation (Matthew 4:1). Of course, He did not succumb to the temptations and commit sin, but He was certainly tempted and that in itself is a degree of demonic influence.

Do you ever take dominion over those forces? To those who *believe*, Jesus gives His authority to cast out demons. Do you ever practice any exorcistic prayer? Do you ask God to cast out a spirit of infirmity that may be causing or aggravating your arthritis, or a spirit of doubt that is inhibiting your faith? Especially if you've had experience with drugs, the occult, astrology, transcendental meditation, reincarnation theories, Eastern religions, et cetera, you have probably been affected by contaminatory forces of evil. Scripture says you can take authority over these things. Do you believe it? If you don't, or if you don't *act* as if you believe it, then your (secondary) faith in the God who revealed it is weak.

Take any one of the doctrinal statements in the Bible, and check your faith by your response to it. The same test can be used with exhortatory texts. For instance, I Corinthians 15:58 encourages us to always abound in the Lord's work for "nothing done for the Lord is ever wasted." Everything we do, every good act we perform, every nickel we give to a poor person is going to have its

53

reward. How about picking up the kids' pajamas, waiting patiently in a traffic jam, preparing a meal, all for the love of God—"nothing you do *for the Lord* is ever wasted." Do you have a headache now? You might pray, "Lord, use this headache to help someone suffering from a migraine someplace, or persons who are being tortured in prison, or use it to enhance the pastoral influence of some clergyman somewhere." Your faith tells you that nothing done for the Lord is wasted. *Nothing.* Is your life permeated with the kind of faith that makes such truths really meaningful for you?

Now, the headache is past, it happened yesterday, it's gone as if it never happened. There is no lingering effect, it's gone and you are the same now as if you hadn't had it at all. The lasting effects of it, however, are in the future, perhaps ten billion years from now you will still be enjoying the higher place in heaven because of how you handled that headache on earth. Why then are we so preoccupied with this little problem now? We are preoccupied with this life and have too little regard for the *next* life. When you look back on your present suffering ten years from now, it will be all forgotten or at least appear less relevant. How will it look 10,000 years from now? Like a star fading away in the distance. You get your sense of perspective from eternity. Do you believe in eternity itself? If you believe it, that's secondary faith. How does it effect your life and everyday behavior? As Paul stated so dramatically in Colossians 3:3, "Have as little desire for things of this world as a dead person does."

In any kind of secondary faith that you touch upon, ask yourself those three inventory questions: Do I *believe*? Do I *really believe*? Do I *act* as if I believe?

Simple questions, but what a difference they could make! "A just man *lives* by faith" (Habakkuk 2:4). Living by faith means living in the heart of God. Paul's injunction needs to be heeded frequently: "*Test* yourself, to see whether you really have faith" (II Corinthians 13:5; cf Romans 12:3).

# Taking A Second Look
# at the Virtue of Faith

**Ask Yourself (Or discuss with a study group)...**

1. What always accompanies scriptural accounts of baptism?

2. Why is personal commitment to Jesus vital in the walk of faith?

3. Why is knowledge about Jesus not enough in itself?

4. What are primary and secondary faith?

5. What makes a good measuring stick for determining the depth of your faith?

6. What is kindergarten spirituality and how do we get beyond it?

7. How do you practice yielding faith?

8. Why does God give us much?

9. How does visualizing Christ in others strengthen our faith?

10. How does harboring resentment interfere with faith's operation?

*Dynamic Three:*

# The Growth Of Faith

On one of our tours to the Holy Land, while crossing the Sea of Galilee, a number of stories were shared by the group, about the place where Peter and Jesus walked upon the water.

One of the stories concerned the Scotsman who came to the Holy Land and wanted to go across the Sea of Galilee to Tiberius. He asked the boatman how much it would cost to go across. The boatmaster replied that it would cost him $100. The Scotsman complained that that seemed an exorbitant price to pay simply to cross the lake by boat. "How come it costs so much?" he asked.

The boatmaster replied, "This is a very special lake. This is where Jesus walked on water."

And the Scotsman said, "At that price, no wonder He walked!"

It was at that special place where Jesus walked upon the water that Peter questioned His appearance: "Lord, if that's really you and not a ghost walking there on the water, bid me come to you" (Matthew 14:28). So Jesus invited him to come. Peter stepped out of the boat (from which we get the term "to step out *in faith*") and began to walk on the water himself (this perhaps being the same occasion of Jesus' water-walking referred to in John 6:18 and 19).

Now try to imagine Peter putting his foot down on the water and testing its astonishing firmness, amazed that it's holding him up. He's walking along and doing fine and starting to feel very confident in his own faith. He's looking at Jesus waiting with outstretched arms. No problems so far.

But then he turns and looks at the heaving waves (which often kick up in the Sea of Galilee when the wind comes channeling down through the valley from the north). He becomes frightened and is sure he's going to be swamped. The moment he looks at the waves and the turbulence around him and takes his eyes off Jesus, he begins to sink. So he cries out, "Lord, save me. I am going to perish!" Jesus reaches down, grasps him by the hand and pulls him up, and then chides him, "Why were you fearful, you man of little faith?"

*Little faith*? He was walking on water! I've never walked on water, so I'm sure Peter had a lot more faith than I have, yet that was little faith, Jesus said. He didn't say Peter had no faith; He said he had little faith. It's the same thing He said to the apostles on another occasion (Matthew 8:26) when they woke Him from His sleep in a storm-tossed boat. They had enough faith to believe that He could do something about the storm; that's why they woke Him up. After Jesus calmed the storm, He chided them: "Why were you fearful, you men of *little* faith?" Again, not *no faith*, just *little faith*. Yet, the very working of that dramatic miracle by Jesus increased their faith, as verse 27 indicates: "Who is this that the wind and sea obey him?"

Why did Jesus in both of these cases talk about *little* faith? He was saying in effect that even if our faith in Him is strong enough to enable us to walk on water and strong enough for us to believe that He could stop a storm

**60**

instantly, it still is not enough. As long as there is an element of fear, anxiety and uncertainty, we have not reached that level of total trust that Jesus wants. With faith, as with the other virtues, we're all in that biggest room in the world, called the room for improvement. The Thessalonian Christians had remarkable faith (I Thessalonians 1:8), yet it continued to grow even more (II Thessalonians 1:3), sustaining them through crushing hardships.

# Horizontal Growth: The "Contagion" of Faith

At deeper levels faith becomes contagious. Jesus speaks to Peter, saying, "Simon, Simon, Satan has asked to sift you like wheat but I have pleaded in prayer for you so that your *faith* should not fail, and when you have repented (of lack of faith) and turned to me again, go strengthen and build up the faith in your brethren" (Luke 22:31 and 32). Build up the faith. Here Jesus implies that one level of faith can be built up to another level. He's talking about growth in faith. If you have little faith, you can have more. If you have much faith, you can have still more (cf. II Peter 1:9; Jude 20). Only when your faith is strong can you help others to grow in their faith. Jesus tells Peter, in effect, "Turn to me to receive, before you turn to your brethren to give."

Paul speaks of this in Philippians 1:25. He felt he was still needed and hence was certain he would be staying on earth a little while longer to help the brethren *grow* and become happy in their faith. He was paralleling Peter's vocation to help people grow from little faith to greater faith. Every really faith-filled person, often unaware of it, subtly exerts a faith-growing influence on others.

My friend's wife has a recipe for "Friendship Cake." The basic ingredient is sourdough yeast starter, which she refers to as her "Herman." It takes but a small amount of Herman to leaven the batter and soon she has enough "Herman-leavened" batter to divide three ways, sharing with two of her friends who do likewise; propagated this way, "Friendship Cakes" have sprung up all across the landscape, each a "descendant" of that small intitial amount of "Herman." That's analagous to the way faith proliferates among the people of God.

Jesus prayed that Peter's faith increase would cause a faith increase in his brethren. When you are near a person of great faith, you pick it up through a sort of spiritual osmosis, especially if you live with them. You will become faith-filled yourself in time. Should you live with a person who is very fearful and has little faith, your faith will tend also to be retarded.

Psychologists speak of a kind of emotional contagion. Thus, a very negative, depressed individual depresses others nearby. A person who is really high and always joyful, optimistic and happy tends to uplift other people. There is a similar contagion in faith. When a person's speech and behavior shouts, "Isn't God good... He loves me so much!", an atmosphere of faith becomes almost palpable, and others quickly detect it. Romans 1:8 describes how widespread this can become. So much of our spirituality is not taught, but *caught*. Paul told Timothy to be faith-fed in order to teach others (I Timothy 4:6). Should you be fortunate to live with a person of deep faith, your faith will grow simply by being in daily contact with that person. If you don't, you may find yourself really struggling to keep your faith alive.

We all need periodically to be uplifted—*faith* lift, if you will excuse the pun. If we don't participate in fellowship and community, we will seldom hear or give an uplifting testimony; there will be little communication of God's presence "horizontally." I tell people in the charismatic renewal that even though they have received the Baptism in the Spirit, if they never go to a prayer meeting they will never hear a good testimony about miracles that happen in other people's lives. They will probably never witness the exercise of the gift of prophecy because prophecies are usually given in community. They will never hear public speaking in tongues (different from praying in tongues) and the accompanying interpretation of tongues. They will hardly ever hear really Spirit-filled, uplifting community singing either in tongues or in the vernacular (Ephesians 5:19; Colossians 3:16; and I Corinthians 14:15). They will never experience through fellowship this enrichment of "holy enthusiasm" as Pope Paul VI called it. One cannot grow in faith *only* by practicing "telephone both spirituality," closing oneself into a closed prayer life with only very private phone calls to God. Thus limited, one's spiritual vitality will not survive. While not neglecting your solitary "inner chamber" prayer (Matthew 6:6), "Do not neglect your prayer meetings as some have done" (Hebrews 10:25).

Jesus formed His own community with the twelve apostles. He shared His last supper, supper being a traditionally family meal, with His "collegium" family, the apostles. Someone has said that human beings are the only animals that do not like to eat alone, they prefer to share a meal. Pope John XXIII said it is true in all ages, especially in our own, that we are saved and sanctified in clusters like grapes. Salvation and sanctification usually operate within the context of community. People go to heaven or hell together. It requires two people to commit adultery, for instance, thereby potentially causing the damnation of not just one but two persons. On the other hand, as St. James points out (James 5:20), if you lead someone away from sin, you not only lead him to salvation but you also predestine your own soul.

We work together for good or for bad. We help or hinder. We cannot avoid communitarian interfacing, even spiritually.

Recognizing that principle, we see that our growth in

faith will depend to a considerable extent on the persons around us just as we may cause their growth in faith. Faith has a way of rubbing off on others. That seems to be implied in I Corinthians 12:7 and 14:26 and many other places where it speaks of togetherness, this community working together to build a faith in the Lord (cf. I Peter 4:10; Ephesians 4:4 and 5).

# Vertical Growth: Fertilizing Faith

All through Scripture we find admonitions to avoid smugness at any level of faith; we should never become self-satisfied but work to increase that faith. The greatest spiritual disease is smugness—the "I'm-good-enough" attitude. "I go to church every Sunday, so I'm a good Christian." That kind of petty mentality does not allow for growth or development. Yet Paul says to be accepting of others whose faith is weak (Romans 14:1). That's what God does with us, in our weakness of faith, for He will not crush the bruised reed nor quench the smouldering flax (Isaiah 42:3). He will not take something that is weak, a dying flame, and let it die out. He will pour fuel on a smouldering fire, as He did through His prayer for Peter's faith-growth (Luke 22:31).

If we take whatever little bit of faith we have and present it to Jesus to work on, He will cause it to develop. In Matthew 25 we read about the talents, different proportions of money loaned to each of three people. The first two invested and doubled it, bringing joy to their master. But the one who did not invest, but buried his money, the master called a worthless, lazy lout and sent him to be punished. He was punished, not for stealing, but for leaving his money to yield no interest. A sin of neglect is sometimes worse than a sin of act (cf. James 4:17).

If we don't develop the faith that is given us, we'll suffer the consequences. If we don't invest and grow in that faith we may become smugly satisfied, claiming that we haven't wasted or lost our faith; we're still practicing our faith, but we've buried it in some way. We will have to render to God an account of our neglected stewardship. God expects us to grow, not simply to stagnate. Letting our faith deteriorate is bad, but letting it grow stagnant isn't much better. "Without faith it is impossible to please God" (Hebrews 11:6). But without *growth* in faith, it is impossible to do God's Will as productive stewards of His gifts.

We all have some degree of faith. We have to learn how to let it grow, and even to make it grow, in the sunlight of God's grace. We do that mainly by living our faith to the fullest. Faith has to be a lived-out thing, invested, involved, activated. Romans 1:17: "The just man will *live* by faith" (cf. Habakkuk 2:4; Galatians 3:11).

Faith will grow if we give it a chance. We don't have to be upset if we notice that we don't have faith that moves mountains. I have really not met anyone with that level of faith. But we might let ourselves feel a bit guilty about the negligent way in which we exercise the faith we have. God may touch us with the realization that we're not really developing our faith, that we're on a kind of faith plateau, living day by day in a routine way. Colossians 2:7 reminds us that just as we had faith to believe in the Lord to save us, now we must go on beyond that to believe in Him to help us handle our many daily problems.

Paul suggests that we give ourselves a test of faith (II Corinthians 13:5): "Do you feel Christ's power and presence more and more within you?" (More and more signifies growth.) "Or are you just pretending to be Christian when actually you aren't at all?" Ask yourself, apply the test to "see if you really be of the faith."

We sometimes feel as if we should be able to do all kinds of miracles at once, like laying hands on the sick to heal them instantly; and if we don't have 100 percent success in getting our prayers answered, we may feel that there is something wrong with our faith. There probably is a defect or limit, but that is no reason to get discouraged. Some people fret because they've never worked a miracle and thus feel that they must have little faith. They are fearful that their faith is actually failing. That is the time to open ourselves humbly to the power of God to develop that faith, as described in I Timothy 3:13: "Develop *bold* faith in the Lord."

If your faith is very weak and you lack boldness in using it, your hesitancy is probably rooted in your fear of failure. That fear could prove fatal to the little faith you might have. Very few people would dare to pray over someone to be healed of blindness, or to pray for the suppression of crime in a particular city, or for the salvation of every prostitute in the nation, but they'll pray for the relief of a headache. They are afraid of becoming discouraged by failing in the big requests, and thus of losing the little faith they have; they then fear they may become unable to obtain even small favors from God that would require less faith.

Yet the Lord does not expect us to attain to mature, fully formed faith all at once (that's why Jesus prayed for Peter's growth in faith). What He does expect of us is a readiness and willingness to grow in faith. A cooperative attitude is a minimum requirement to "develop bold faith in the Lord." Without our cooperation, we could become spiritually apathetic, and that can be a real problem. The "don't-rock-the-boat" attitude, or general disinterest in faith-growth, is not merely a mental state of mind, but a disastrous prelude to spiritual deterioration, for "all that is not of faith is sin" (Romans 14:23).

# God's Operation

God wants us to *expect* to grow in faith. So let's talk about the avenues through which we can look for this growth. How can we fertilize the faith we already have? First, there is God's part in faith building, and then there is our part.

God's part works in several ways. He wants us, first of all, to know that faith comes from Him as a gift (Acts 3:16; I Corinthians 12:9), and that He is the builder of our faith (Hebrews 12:2; John 17:19). Realizing that He both gives and develops our faith opens us to growth. Jesus pleads (John 14:1), "Believe in God; believe in me." This starts the growth process.

The second step in God's operation of cultivating faith is to teach us through experience. Our faith is fed when we see God intervene dramatically in our own or others' lives. Before I became involved in the charismatic renewal, I had some level of faith. But after witnessing a crescendo of extraordinary healings and other events, and after hearing countless amazing testimonies, my level of faith has grown. It has been fertilized by what I've seen happening in the lives of these people. It is now easier to believe not just that God *could* do it but that He *would* do it, not just that He *can* do it but that He *will* do it. I didn't have that kind of faith ten years ago, or even three years ago, as much as I have it now. I have come to expect God to work miracles and the hope of my own faith increasing (II Corinthians 10:15). When I open my mail and read almost daily of someone being healed, or a marriage that was near divorce now featuring a couple madly in love, I come to expect such divine interventions. It is no longer a rare thing. Through these experiences, my faith is built.

We come to have more faith in the person of Jesus as we read and meditate on the miracles of Jesus. Contemporaneously, as we see the power of God operating intimately (even though subtly) in our life, and then focus on Jesus as the cause of that, we come to grow in our faith in Him. From an event-oriented observation we arrive at a person-oriented faith. In the words of Jesus (John 14:11): "At least believe in me because of the works I perform."

A third way in which the Lord works at building our faith is directly. God directly imparts the charismatic gift of faith to us, particularly after receiving the Baptism in the Spirit. Or, He may impart astonishing faith during times of deep contemplative prayer, when He seems to speak to us in a very clear way. Paul implies this in Colossians 1:9: "Ask God to make you wise about spiritual things. Thus, you will come to know God better and better."

The more we come to know the Lord directly, and experience His reality (Ephesians 3:19), the more we will exercise our faith. God will start to work minor miracles in our life "rewarding our faith with His power" (II Thessalonians 1:11). Dozens of times a day we begin to notice happy and exciting, yet extraordinary "coincidences," and these start occurring with increasing frequency. They are God's whisperings of love for us, spawned by our growth in faith. For instance, a tax rebate arrives in the mail when you need it most, or a much desired item is found at a super bargain price. Such "little things" become commonplace and almost staggering in their consistent occurrence. This builds our person-oriented faith in the Lord because it is as if God were saying, "See? I am taking care of you because I *love* you!"

In summary, the three main ways God develops our faith are by responding to our God-centered trust, by granting us experiences of extraordinary or miraculous things happening in our life, and finally by directly and sovereignly imparting His faith to us (often mainfested by extraordinary "coincidences"). In these three ways, God reaches us to stimulate our growth in faith. So much for God's part in the process.

# Our Cooperation

Let us now look at the other side of the coin—not at what God does, but at what we can do to cooperate with His grace in the building of faith.

The first thing we can do is listen to or read and meditate on the Word of God. Romans 10:17 says faith comes by hearing the Word of God. There are still some so-called Christians who really don't accept it (cf. verse 16). They somehow think they are going to grit their teeth and exercise their faith without opening the Bible. They either refuse or neglect to read God's love letter, God's Word. They faithfully use their little prayer books and their little prayer rituals, but they think they don't need the Bible. Jesus' challenging question to the Sadducees He also addresses to these Christians: "Don't you ever read the Scriptures?" (Matthew 22:31). He asked the same question of the Pharisees (Luke 6:3).

The Bible itself tells us that "Scripture makes us wise to accept God's salvation by believing (having trust and faith) in Christ Jesus. The whole Bible was given by inspiration of God and is useful to teach us what is true and to make us realize what is wrong in our lives. It straightens us out and helps us do what is right. It is *God's way* of making us well prepared at every point, *fully equipped* to do good" (II Timothy 3:15-17).

Paul says in Philippians 1:25 that we should "grow and be happy and fulfilled in our faith"; and we should want to use every tool God has given us to make that happen. In Romans 10:17 we are told that a major tool for this purpose is openness to the Scriptures—hearing the Word of God. You may hear something of God's Word in sermons, but of course sermons vary widely in their content. Many are "cotton candy" homilies—sermons with little or no scriptural substance. You take a big bite and suddenly after a moment of sweetness, there is very little left to nourish you. So you may have to look elsewhere for God's word. *It is always available in the Bible.*

All of Psalm 119 is about the Word of God: "Cheer me, Lord, with your word, build me up with your word" (verse 28). "Your words are a torch to light the path ahead of me so I will not stumble and fall. Your words enlighten me" (verse 105). "My heart stands in awe of your word" (verse 161).

If you don't have a familiarity with the Word of God and truly love it (verse 16), your faith will not grow very much. You will hit a low plateau of faith and stay at that level the rest of your life. Devotional materials are beautiful, yet I never cease to be amazed at the shallowness of people who read all kinds of devotional literature *exclusively*. They are constantly receiving a "secondhand" word of God— only in the most remote and therefore, diluted way. Some spend hours reading about all kinds of apparitions, visions, etc., but they won't spend five minutes a day reading the Bible. They practice upsidedown Christianity; their value system is warped. They remain way out on the far edges of the circle and they spend little time at the center of the circle, in the primary content of Christian experience. They don't meaningfully relate to God in His primary revelation, His Word. They may spend hours praying to overcome anxiety or illness while ignoring Psalm 119:165: "Great peace is had by those who love your word; and *they shall have no sickness."*

A second way to build faith is by allowing God to make His presence felt through the charismatic gifts, especially prophecy. How many persons really open themselves to hear the gift of prophecy operating? In I Corinthians 14:22, Paul says prophecy (not necessarily futuristic events) is what Christians need. Unbelievers aren't ready for it; their faith isn't deep enough. He says an unsaved person or one *without the charismatic gifts* upon hearing tongues is likely to think the tongues-speaker is crazy (I Corinthians 14:23). But on the other hand, he says, if you exercise prophecy ( a gift higher than the gift of tongues) and that same unspiritual person comes into the prayer assembly, the prophecies (messages from God) will convince him of the fact that he is a sinner and his conscience will be pricked. "As he listens, his secret thoughts will be laid bare and he will fall down on his knees and worship God and declare that God is really there among you." This, then, is another way that God projects His presence to stimulate faith—through the charismatic gift of prophecy, authentically used.

As God speaks to us through Scripture as a form of public revelation, He speaks to us also through prophecy as a form of private revelation (and, of course, the gift of discernment is to be used to determine the authenticity of each prophecy). Our faith is thus stimulated by public (scriptural) revelation and well-discerned private (prophetic) revelation.

I remember hearing a very "high-octane" prophecy from a person who was clearly a genuine prophet—not just a person with a gift of prophecy, but with a well-developed ministry of prophecy. With over a thousand people present at this charismatic Mass, this fellow stood and spoke a couple of simple sentences of prophecy of God, referring to His love for us. It was incredibly powerful and left a perceptible impact on everyone there—probably more effective than a hundred sermons in its power of conviction. I'm sure everyone there was given a surge of faith that had long-lasting effects. Today, years later, people still speak about that short prophecy. Faith, especially faith in God's love for us (I John 4:16 and Romans 5:5) can be enormously expanded through prophecy (I Corinthians 14:24 and 25).

This leads to the third way that we can fertilize our faith, namely by allowing our faith to "work through love" (Galatians 6:5). The acme of faith is the yielding faith that believes in God's personal love for each of us— the "Good News" or gospel message. Once you *really believe* that God loves you (I John 4:16), and you relax in His arms, *nothing disturbs you!* No anxiety, no loneliness, no fear, because you *know* He can and will make "all things work together for good" (Romans 8:28). Your faith convinces you that God created you because He loves you, and He heals you because He loves you. We learn to *count* on His love and that itself is a faith-building experience. Pope Paul VI reminded us that to receive God's hug is to surrender to His personal, merciful love. Faith induces this experience of divine intimacy, for "faith works through love."

As we become aware not only of God's love for us but His promised ongoing presence (Matthew 28:20) as "Emmanuel" (Matthew 1:25; Isaiah 7:14), our faith in and dependency on Him will grow. This enables us to "Live in vital union with him" (Colossians 2:6). We can then say with Paul (Galatians 2:20), "I live, but not I, it is Christ who lives in me" as we experience His divinity penetrating our humanity. Paul is not saying Christ is near him, or with him, or that he is following Christ. Paul is saying that Christ is living his life, totally permeating him and all his activities. When we reach that point we are operating at a very high level of faith, especially when we're truly convinced of the very personal dimension of God's unitive love. St. Augustine wrote: "God loves each one of us as if there were only one of us." Yielding to this faithbuilding truth found in God's Word will enable us to recognize that Christ is in us through the power of His Spirit—in us in the deepest way. At that point our faith becomes a truly mystical, contemplative experience.

Paul asks if we *know* we are the temples of God wherein His Spirit dwells (the word "know" in Scripture usually means experiential knowledge). "Don't you know (*experience*) that you are the temple of God?" (I Corinthians 3:16). He is not asking, don't you acknowledge the theological truth that you are the temple of God? That is not the question. The question is, do you *experience* that within you? "Glorify and bear God in your bodies" (I Corinthians 6:20) as well as your souls. He's talking about an experienced reality.

Fourth, we can *pray* for faith as the apostles did (Luke 17:5): "Lord, increase our faith." After all, "The Lord is the author and finisher of our faith" (Hebrews 12:2). He's the source and the end, the alpha and omega (Revelations 1:11). We turn to Him knowing that the Lord wants us to have faith and that He will generously give it to us as He supplies all our needs (cf. Acts 14:17). We should pray to be lifted up to that next level of faith, while asking also that any gaps in our faith be filled up. The "'Lord-I-know-you-*can*" prayer of faith then becomes a "Lord-I-know-you-*will*" prayer.

Fifth, be willing to *act* in faith. Good works affirm and authenticate our faith (James 2:17). Neglect of good works is ultimately neglect of Christ ("If you neglect to do it unto one of the least of these my brethern, you neglect to do it unto me." Matthew 15:45). James says faith without good works is dead (James 2:17). It takes a tremendous act of faith to see and relate to Christ in your fellow man. If you look at a skid row derelict merely as a repulsive person, your faith is retarded. To see instead the precious dignity and nobility of that skid row derelict created in the image of God and destined for heaven— something incredibly awesome—requires faith in large measure. To *act* towards that person, using that "insight", requires even greater faith.

You can't practice charity if you don't have faith. Only the eyes of faith allow you to see the Christ presence in a wino—or even to see the Christ presence in someone you live with who gets on your nerves. It takes deep faith to look beyond the shadow to this substance, and see a precious soul redeemed by Christ. You can't *act* on faith without first *having* faith. That is, you can't perform good works if you don't first have faith to activate the charity. Faith is the basic virtue in life's struggles, for I John 5:4 says, "Our victory over the world is through our faith." Peter speaks about this whole idea of active, operational faith enhanced by its "additions": "To obtain these gifts, you need *more than faith*, you must also work hard to be good, you must learn to know God better, discover what He wants you to do (God's will). You must learn to put aside you own desires so you become patient and godly, gladly letting God have His way with you (holy

73

abandonment). That will make the next step possible which is freedom to enjoy other people and to like them and finally grow to love them dearly. The more you go on this way the more you will grow strong spiritually and become fruitful and useful to our Lord Jesus Christ. Anyone who fails to go after these additions is blind indeed, or at least very shortsighted, and has forgotten that God delivered him from the old life of sin. But now we can live a strong, good new life for the Lord" (II Peter 1:3-9). Faith has to be implemented, Peter seems to be saying.

As we experience each of these many, many realities of divine revelation, we have opportunities for faith-building reactions. They all are sustained by familiarity with God's Word. If these tremendous truths are neglected, they grow dim and fade through disuse. But through reading God's Word and dwelling on His Word, these truths remain fresh and activated in our minds. Turning the diamond of His truth around daily and studying its many facets, its irridesence, opalesence and variations of color, our faith is fortified.

Take, for instance, the gift of praying in tongues (one of the four biblically-support ways of using that gift). You can't receive the gift of tongues without faith. When it first begins, it usually is not a language, only prayerful babbling. It is an articulated vehicle for mental prayer of praise (I Corinthians 14:14); it takes *faith* to develop it into a prayer language. After it does develop, it becomes more beautiful, more yielding, far more enriching. And its prayerful use builds more faith (Romans 8:26 and 27). The same is true in the more ordinary areas of our lives, where faith is needed. Consider, for instance, the problem of fear-control. God usually doesn't want us to be afraid. Jesus tells Jairus not to fear but to trust Him to raise his daughter from death (Mark 5:36). On more than a few occasions He tells His apostles to "fear not." "Do not worry (have anxiety or fear) about what you are going to eat and wear," Jesus commands. Heathens, He says, worry about material things; authentic Christians do not (Matthew 6:32). Try giving yourself a "faith score" on the basis of your freedom from worry, anxiety or fear.

It is important to remember not to try to "work up" your feelings of faith but to look to the Lord to do it for you. The harder you try to create faith, the less you will succeed. It is important also to watch your *focus* of faith. For instance, trying to develop faith to believe your prayers will be answered, you might be developing faith in your faith, but not in Jesus Christ; only in that focus will faith "restore the soul" (Hebrews 10:39).

There was a little leaflet anonymously written back in the thirties called "The Golden Key", and translated into hundreds of languages. The whole idea of this very successful little booklet was: don't look at the waves, look at Jesus on the waves. Don't focus on your faith or on solving the problem, focus on Jesus, excepting Him to solve it. Our faith must become person-oriented, not problem-oriented.

Many people are problem-oriented individuals. When they are doing nothing, problems occupy their minds. While washing dishes or cooking a meal, their thoughts may turn to worrying about a sick husband or a financial problem or an alcoholic family member. This automatically sets limits to the depth of one's faith, since it is problem-oriented thinking. Such thinking may not only stop the growth of faith; it may even diminish faith, and "those who shrink back in their faith give no pleasure to the Lord" (Hebrews 10:38).

But if that problem is used as the stimulus to focus on the Lord as able and willing to solve the problem, the thoughts become Jesus-oriented and the solution to the problem is within reach. The "golden key" is to have faith in Jesus, not faith in your prayer, or faith in your faith.

I wasted many years trying to develop my feelings of assurance that I was going to get an answer to prayer, rather than cultivating a personal faith in Christ. It finally dawned on me that I was using the wrong approach. My faith had been faith-oriented, not Jesus-oriented. We grow in faith not merely by looking within ourselves, but by looking to Christ, depending on Him, His power, His goodness, His love, His promises with a reckless abandon. Psalm 119:114: "*Your* promises are my hope."

One of the greatest challenges in prayer is to ask for things with real expectancy, not mere urgency in begging the Lord. "Do not have anxiety about anything, but present your needs to the Lord in supplication and thanksgiving. *Then* you will have the peace that passes all understanding" (Philippians 4:7).

I often give people this test of faith: Suppose you receive a call asking you to come to the emergency room at the hospital because your child has just been hit by a car. He's dying, his skull is crushed. Do you play the radio and sing a song on the way to the hospital? Of course not; your entire attention is on prayer. What are you saying while praying on the way? "*God, don't let that child die!*" You're begging, pleading for Him to save that child's life. There's anxiety there, and that is what Paul tells us to avoid. Rather, you should be saying, "*Lord, you know what I want—I want to save that child's life, but Lord, if you want to take that child to heaven, go ahead. Not my will, but thine be done. And thank you for your decision in this matter.*" You've presented your need without begging, but with real supplication and thanksgiving. There is no anxiety in that prayer. A truly critical situation like this will provide an acid test for your faith and trust in God and His goodness—no matter how the situation turns out.

What would our prayer have been had we been in St. Stephen's sandals when he was stoned to death? Undoubtedly most of us would have felt justified in asking to be delivered from the murderous mob. Ours might even have been the prayer of panic, "Oh God, help me! Save me from death!"

But what was Stephen's prayer? "Lord Jesus, receive my spirit" (Acts 7:59)—expressing calm assurance of the Lord's welcoming embrace like Jesus on Calvary ("Father, into thy hands..."). And then he had the faith-filled love to pray for his executioners! "Lord, lay not this sin to their charge"—the mighty prayer of faith that acknowledged the belief that God was in control; Stephen truly believed he was about to be ushered through the gates of Glory. It was not a panic-prayer, but an anxiety-free faith-prayer that Paul—one of his executioners— would later describe, after his conversion, in Philippians 4:7.

Expansive confidence is another characteristic of deep faith. Paul says in Ephesians 1:19, "How incredibly great His power is to help those who *believe* in him." Two chapters later (Ephesians 3:20) he says, "This mighty power at work within us is able to do far more than we would ever dare to ask or even dream of—infinitely beyond our highest prayers, desires, thoughts or hopes!" But we don't usually tap into that power because we don't pray with faith-spawned confidence. We're going to this spiritual billionaire and we're saying, "God, can you spare a dime?" God has *limitless* riches and power and wants to give us so much and we, in effect, embarrass Him by asking for so little. It is not only a kind of insult to God, but an implicit acknowledgement of just how weak our faith really is. We don't develop our faith by being reluctant to lean on Him. Prayer itself should manifest *an act of faith*, not a *lack* of faith.

Some 700 students at Brown University in Rhode Island petitioned the Student Health Services to stockpile cyanide suicide pills for use in case of nuclear war. One student called the request "a very American way to handle moral problems." Where is there any hope, any joy, any faith in such an attitude? Many Christians have a similar suicidal hopelessness in their prayer because their faith is anemic.

Resist a spirit that goes against faith. I Peter 5:9 says, "Resist steadfast in the faith the spirit of fear and the spirit of doubt." There are a lot of evil spirits attacking us today, be it divorce or resentment or faithlessness or depression or addiction to nicotine or alcohol. Evil spirits are actually oppressing good people. As Monsignor Walsh writes in his book *The Key to the Charismatic Renewal in the Catholic Church*, even the holiest of people, even the most spiritual person can be assailed by the devil and his demons. Evil spirits of infirmity, of anger, or of anxiety can actually attach themselves to us and superimpose themselves on weak areas of the body or the mind. And some people never pray for deliverance from them, even though Jesus in teaching the Lord's Prayer commands us to ask God to "deliver us from the evil one."

Certain spirits go against faith— the spirits of faithlessness, fear, doubt. They can drag us down and prevent miracles from ever happening in our lives. "And he did not do many miracles there because of their lack of faith" (Matthew 13:58). There are miracles Jesus will not work in the midst of unbelief. I Peter 5:9 says to resist steadfast in the faith. We must deal vigorously with those spirits that militate against the faith (cf. James 4:2).

"Cast your anxieties on the Lord...Satan roams about like a roaring lion seeking whom he will devour. Be firm *in your faith* against him." Paul says something similar when he speaks of putting on the armor of God so that we might stand up against the devil's evil attacks. We are not fighting human beings, we are fighting cosmic powers of darkness. Especially watch for a spirit that seeks to undermine your faith, suggesting: "You've never worked a miracle, so give up." Satan will try to persuade you not to use faith and not to develop your faith. He will tell you it's just for very holy people, but not for you. He will do everything he can to disuade you from growing in faith.

Go to where your faith can be fed, especially Christian gatherings. It is difficult to grow in your faith by yourself.

Get into prayer meetings, groups, retreats and organizations where you can have your faith fed. Tapes and the right kind of books, especially Holy Scripture, are a great help too.

The true story is told of a shipload of Spanish conquistadors who were shipwrecked off the coast of South America. Only three men survived, floating for days on a makeshift raft without food or water. Nearly bereft of hope, they at last sighted land in the distance. With all the feeble strength they could muster, they paddled for the land. Weaker and weaker they became from dehydration until they collapsed just off shore. Each morning they could barely open their eyes to watch natives come down to the shoreline, dip their hands in the water and drink. The miserable men on the raft could not believe their eyes. Surely they were hallucinating for no man can drink only seawater and live.

Finally one morning, first one and then another of the conquistadors died and were nudged overboard by the lone survivor. He peered once more at the daily ritual of the natives coming down to the sea to drink. Though certain it would be the death of him, the last conquistador crawled to the edge of the raft and dipped his hands into the sea. The water was sweet. He and his shipwrecked companions had discovered the mouth of the mighty Amazon River where eleven billion gallons of fresh water per second rush to meet the sea. The last man lived because he finally believed. The other two died because they would not.

Jesus offers the sweet water of life eternal to all who will drink. So many needlessly wither and die spiritually just a sip away from faith-enriched spiritual fulfillment. Let us pray with the apostles, "Lord, increase our faith!"

# Taking a Second Look
# at the Growth of Faith

**Ask Yourself (Or discuss with a study group)...**

1. Where does the term "to step out in faith" come from?

2. Is "little faith" a good or bad sign regarding Christian maturity?

3. What is the greatest spiritual disease?

4. In what ways do we bury our faith?

5. How are we taught through experiences?

6. How does faith grow through people in our lives?

7. In what ways does "telephone booth spirituality" stifle growth?

8. In what ways does God let us know He is taking care of us?

9. In what primary ways can we cooperate with the building of our faith?

10. What does it mean to "act in faith"?

11. What is the difference between confident prayer and the prayer of panic?

12. How does a spirit of fear cripple our Christianity?

13. How can faith best be fed?

*Dynamic Four:*

# The Prayer of Faith

The media are missing the biggest and saddest story of all time and it's right under their noses. An intuitive newspaper editor shouldn't hesitate to print this headline on tomorrow's front page:

## "AMERICA SUFFERS TERRIBLE FAMINE"

No, not famine of food and water, but a horrible, shriveling, killing famine of faith in the Word of God. The prophet Amos wrote the headline thousands of years ago: "Behold, the days will come, says the Lord God, when I will send a famine in the land, not a famine of bread, nor a thirst for water, but of hearing the words of the Lord..."(Amos 8:11).  Meant for Israel, yes, but it is not the only nation that is hard-of-hearing. In every country, too few are hearing God's words. The Bible could be subtitled The Book of Faith, but it takes a believer to activate that faith, to hear and to *act*.

There was a self-service elevator with a sign on the control panel pointing to the eighth floor button that read: "The eighth floor button is out of order." Some wag had written beneath it: "Instead, push numbers 3 and 5."

There is no substitute for certain things. The third and fifth floors do not substitute for the eighth floor. And there is no substitute for faith. We are reminded in Hebrews 11:6 that without faith it is *impossible* to please God. He who comes to God must *believe* that He is and that He is a rewarder of those who seek Him. There is no substitute for that. It is the criterion that determines how we grow in our spiritual life.

We have natural faith. Every time you mail a letter, you believe the letter is going to reach its destination. There is no proof that it will. You have a total confidence that when you let go of that letter and it slips into the mailbox, it will go where you want it to go. There is a *letting go* involved, and that's a kind of faith in itself.

Natural faith operates all the time. You put catsup on your food that you have never had chemically analyzed. Yet you assume that it is not full of strychnine and you believe the ones who bottled it did not attempt to poison the contents. The certitude is so great that it follows through with action. When you walk across the street on a green light, you cross in front of powerful cars with idling motors. You *believe* the motorists won't run you down. You take an action of trust so great, you actually place your life in the hands of others.

When you undergo surgery, how do you *know* the surgeon isn't simply going to stab you? When you are under anesthesia, you are completely trusting in the surgeon's skill. The difference between a stab and a surgical incision is the difference between evil intentions and good ones. You presume he intends good. That's a real act of faith.

When you enter an elevator, you have faith to believe the inspectors saw to it that the cables were strong enough to hold you up. If you had a doubt, you wouldn't get in. You have enough faith in the architect of the building you live in, to believe that the roof is strong enough not to cave in.

You act on that belief by putting yourself in a position that shows you believe by living there.

Every time you get a haircut, how do you know you aren't going to get scalped? You trust the barber. You trust the airline pilot to take you to Houston, believing you won't end up in Chicago (or Cuba).

You never saw Abraham Lincoln but you trust historians who say that he lived, and even celebrate a holiday in his memory. That belief expresses itself in action. Our whole life functions on the basis of natural faith. It would be impossible to go one hour without exercising natural faith.

## Supernatural Faith

Likewise in the spiritual life, we cannot do anything without faith, most especially in prayer. Without it, we certainly can't please God (Hebrews 11:6). Only Christians can have true supernatural faith, based on the promises of Jesus, through the revelation of God's Word. Faith means giving substance to, or substantiating, the things hoped for, the things that are not seen (Hebrews 11:1). This faith is not inherent in human nature. In terms of salvation, it is God's grace freely given (Ephesians 2:8).

What is an adequate basis for the prayer of faith? We can say what it is not. It is not the evidence of outward circumstances. Elijah prayed for rain when there was no rain in sight. Six times came the report that the sky was cloudless (I Kings 18). Regardless, Elijah insisted that rain was on the way. It was—in torrents. Yet there was no external confirmation for that belief when the prayer of faith went up. This is belief and trust in God, *in spite of appearances*. I can't tell you how important that statement is, to believe and trust in God in spite of appearances. It looks like this person you are praying for is unconvertible. It looks like that cancer is irreversible. It looks like that child of yours is going to be an alcoholic, and nothing is going to change it. All the evidence goes against what you want. To believe in God despite appearances is what triggers the miracle. Not to rely on your faith, but to rely on God.   There are a number of people who believe when probability is in their favor, but faith acts when the probabilities are minimal. That is why faith is so uplifting; it carries an optimism within itself.

Secondly, faith does not require or demand a sign to shore it up. When Jesus was on the cross, those berating Him challenged Him to come down from the cross and save himself if He was indeed the Christ. They wanted a sign. If He had come down, they would have believed.He would have had converts right there on the spot. It would have been an overwhelming miracle. There was nothing more faithless than that very challenge itself.

Remember the two thieves crucified with Jesus? The one said, "Save yourself and save us if you are the Messiah." But the good thief responded, "We don't deserve to be saved. This man does, He is innocent." He did not demand a sign. Gideon's putting out a fleece was to determine the will of God. It was not God's response to Gideon's request that made that miracle happen.It was a sort of concession to the feebleness of Gideon's faith rather than a reward for the strength of his faith.

Jesus constantly deprecated the seeking of a sign, the "prove-it-to-me" attitude. The Jewish leaders demanded a sign of Jesus. Jesus replied that His sign was the temple would be destroyed by them in three days and He would raise it up again, speaking of His body (John 2:18 and 19). The Pharisees desired to test Jesus' claim to be Messiah. They asked Him to give some great demonstration in the skies. He said in effect that they are their own worst sign, an evil and *unbelieving* generation that would receive no further sign except for a miracle that had already happened, that of John (Matthew 16:1-4). On another occasion (Matthew 12:39) Jesus said that only an evil, *faithless* generation would ask for further proof.

After my first visit to Europe, I wrote a book telling of all the extraordinary things I had seen in two months. Things like the incorrupt bodies of unembalmed saints almost as fresh as the day they died, and the three days I spent with the stigmatic Padre Pio, serving his Mass and watching the blood fall from his hands on the altar. People who read my book wrote back and said they'd never heard of miracles like that, *ongoing* miracles. For some, their faith was stimulated and they decided to return to the sacraments. Their faith was dependent upon signs. As long as they could hear that miracles were going on, they felt they ought to believe. Yet Jesus called that kind of person *faithless* because they possess a posterior faith, the sort that believes *because* of a miracle rather than *causing* it. The person who can say "That's interesting but I don't need this kind of thing" is the person of faith.

When Louis IX was King of France, some of his courtiers came to him and told him to come quickly to witness a miracle; the Christ Child had appeared in the palace chapel standing on the altar next to the tabernacle. To their amazement, the king refused to go. He told them he did not need to go to the chapel to see the miracle because he knew that Jesus was present there all the time. He refused to go to see the apparition because he had tremendous faith. Blessed are those *who do not see* and yet believe, Jesus told doubting Thomas (John 20:29). Real faith does not depend on signs, but often triggers them.

Nor does faith depend on feelings or emotional reactions. The basis of your prayer of faith isn't whether or not you feel good. You're not assured of your salvation because you "feel" saved. True faith is in the Savior, not in saved feelings. Faith is independent of feelings. If you feel very unprayerful, without much fervor, and still you pray, then you have the faith of a sterling character; and grace is flooding into your soul far more at that time than if you were to pray only when you felt like it.

So, many things faith is not. So what *is* it really? Where does faith find its warranty? It is warranted simply in the promises of the Word applied to our hearts by the Spirit of God. It is divinely given intuition, an assurance that God has answered our prayer. *Faith is an effortless confidence in God.*

## Faith's Simplicity

When a husband and wife are deeply in love with each other, there is no effort required in trusting each other. If you are truly close to the Lord, faith in Him becomes effortless. It is a kind of leaning on Him, with a peace and security.

One time I was praying for some people for healing and right in the middle of that healing session I was straining and gripping the person's head and relying somehow on physical effort to bring about this miracle. Suddenly, in the midst of my teeth-gritting efforts, the Lord just seemed to speak and say, *"I'll* do it!"

I was acting as if I were doing it, that somehow I was the healer. But I'm not the healer, the Lord is the healer. When that realization hit me, I said, "Lord, take over. Just use my hands as your hands. I can't heal cancer and blindness and such things, Lord. Just channel all your healing love through me."

It changed my entire mentality. At that moment God made me realize I had been doing it the wrong way. I was making it effortful rather than effortless. The closer you get to the Lord, the more you lean on Him with reckless abandon, the less effort it requires to practice faith, for real faith is a form of *surrender.*

It is not necessary to scream and yell to heal or to cast out demons. Just a simple faith.

I saw a man once conferring the Baptism of the Holy Spirit. He was laying hands on a person and commanding them to receive the Holy Spirit. Sweat was pouring down his face and he was gripping the person tightly, squinting mightily and grinding his teeth; expending vast amounts of energy. I couldn't help but wonder if the man was baptizing in the Spirit, or was it the Lord? St. John the Baptist said Jesus was the one that baptizes in the Spirit; we simply administer the prayerful act. And the same is true of the other gifts of the Spirit. He is the one who does it.

It is important to distinguish between the natural desires and the real promptings of the Holy Spirit behind your prayer of faith. Again, I John 5:14 speaks of the confidence that we have before Him that if we ask anything according to His will, He hears us. And if we *know* that He hears us, the request will be granted.

The prayer of faith then is a definite request in line with God's will, made with definitive faith for a definite answer—and presuming you have it, simply stepping out and claiming it.

# Anointed Faith

Now there is a certain type of situation where you need to have an anointing, particularly when dealing with really "high-voltage" types of miracles. Walking on water, for instance. When Peter walked on the water, it was in response to a prompting to come forward from Jesus Himself. Suppose he had tried to walk on water the day before or after the miracle? What do you think would have happened to Peter? He would have sunk like a rock. Why? Because he received a special anointing at a special moment, a call, a personal invitation from the Lord Himself. The other apostles couldn't walk on water because they didn't get the call. When the anointing is there, then the faith that is activated by that anointing is there and that is especially true for very extraordinary miracles.

When God's Word is meant for limited situations or persons, it's called "rhema"; otherwise, it's "logos". For example, the Bible says sell all and give to the poor and follow Jesus. That's a "rhema". If everyone did that, they would have no way to support their families or enjoy homes, and they would be impoverished. However, if the Lord *called* you to evangelical poverty as He did St. Francis of Assisi, then there would be an *anointing*. If the Lord called you to exercise faith for a mountain-moving miracle, then the anointing would accompany that faith. You can cause a disaster if you don't know about the anointing for certain kinds of miracles—if you were to interpret a "rhema" as a "logos".

There was a young priest who read the passage in Matthew 10:8 that says go out and cure the lepers and the blind and raise the dead—clearly a "rhema" passage. As he had a funeral that day, the priest went to the undertaker's parlor and in the presence of all the family and the mourners told them to pray with him that the deceased would arise! Peter did it, Paul did it, and many saints performed that miracle of raising people from the dead. The young priest felt he could do it, too, if he exercised his faith.

He walked over to the corpse and laid hands on it. The family stood about totally bewildered. It would be terrifying if the deceased did sit up in the coffin and yet a joy if he did. They didn't know whether to have anticipated joy or fear or hesitancy—in short, they were torn with all these conflicting emotions. The priest said to the corpse, "In the name of Jesus Christ, I command you to rise from the dead!" But he had no anointing to do that and nothing happened. There was no inner positive assurance and so his faith was not a substantiated faith, but simply wishful thinking. It certainly was not a matter of aligning himself with God's will. He didn't ask to know whether it was God's will to raise that person from the dead. All he said was, "I'm assuming it is God's will."

The result was that the faith of the family and friends gathered was shattered. They left nervous wrecks, a heavy guilt trip laid on everyone. They figured they, too, must not have had enough faith. Secondly, they now doubted the Word of God to be true because it says to go out and raise the dead and here it hadn't worked. All because of the imprudence of acting without the anointing or the full gospel message that the anointing and the certitude must be present.

The first step of faith is asking God what His will is and praying, "Thy will be done." First we must pray to be shown God's will, and only then can we believe He will do it.

There was a Mrs. Horton who had faith, not as deep as it could have been, but a devout lady nonetheless. Her husband died without having provided for her livelihood, leaving her almost destitute. She prayed with what she thought was faith that some miracle might happen whereby she could keep the house she was so sentimentally attached to after all the years of having lived there. Financially, she had to sell that house to survive, or so she thought. She prayed that God would cause something to happen that she would not have to sell. In praying for this, she didn't ask for God's will or faith to know God's will. She simply prayed that she wouldn't have to sell the house.

Nothing happened and a few months later she had to sell. Cleaning out the attic in preparation for the sale, she found an old, old stamp collection that had been in her husband's family for many years. She almost threw it on a pile of rubbish but finally she put it aside to save. A year later when she moved into a smaller apartment, she was still bitter because God hadn't answered her prayer. She had loved that house.

One day she happened to see a newspaper listing of the value of certain stamps. She remembered that stamp collection she had saved, found it and took it to the stamp dealer. She walked out of that store with a check for $11,000. Then she realized that that old house had been too big for her anyway. God had taken away the burden of having to care for it; and she now had enough money to pay her expenses. What had appeared to be her unanswered prayer turned out to be an answered prayer. Sometimes our plans fail in order that God's plans for us might succeed.

Including death. We pray for healing and God gives us death instead, the ultimate healing. Pray for faith that believes basic truths like Romans 8:28: "To those who love God, all things work together for good." Such faith is much deeper than that which says, "Lord, I know you're going to heal me." It is the faith that can say, "Lord, if you don't heal me, whatever is going to happen is going to be for the best. If you do heal me, then that's for the best."

# Success Through Faith

The chief ingredient in successful prayer is faith. In James 1:5 he says, "If you want to know what *God* wants (not what you want), ask Him. He will gladly tell you. He is always ready to give a bountiful supply of wisdom to all who ask Him. He will not resent it. But when you ask Him, be sure you really expect Him to tell you. If you don't ask with faith, don't expect the Lord to give you a really solid answer." An answer to what? An answer to your prayer for healing? Not necessarily. Rather an answer to know God's will, the wisdom to know what to do. Then you can pray for your needs as we are taught in I John 5:14, *in accordance with His will.*

I know of a six-month-old baby who had a club foot, which is a bone malformation. The baby obviously could not make an act of faith for healing, but the mother could. And so could the priest who prayed with her over the phone. They prayed together, and overnight the baby's leg was normalized. The doctors at the UCLA Medical

Center were absolutely amazed. The before and after X-rays looked like those of two different children, one normal, the other abnormal.

A kind of preamble to faith is knowledge that God wants perhaps a radical miracle healing, rather than a healing through surgery or the other so-called natural "miracles" of technology, science and medicine. Ecclesiasticus 38 says, "...all healing is from God...a wise man will not despise God's medicines...there is a time when you must fall into the hands of doctors and they should beseech the Lord that he will bless what they prescribe to relieve and cure your ailments." The interweaving of human and divine actions often occurs in the healing process. The faith that you ask for to know God's will in this regard might be to not only know if God wants you cured, but also to know if God wants you to pray for a radical miracle cure or for correction through standard medical procedure.

So faith ultimately is not simply believing you'll get what you want, independently of what God wants, but rather a seeking of God's will in order to adjust your faith-prayer to fit His plan—especially for deeply serious things such as the healing of a retarded child.

For the most part, you can say that God always wants spiritual healing. If your son or daughter has left the Church and turned away from God, you can be sure God wants to bring that person aback to Himself. Of course, it is God's will that that soul be saved. We know that.

But in other situations there are things we don't know. The prayer should include a petition for the faith to know the direction (answer) we ought to seek.

A couple with a retarded child came to one of my retreats. The amniocentesis test prior to the child's birth showed the couple would have a child with Down's Syndrome. The doctor had wanted to abort the mongoloid fetus. The couple resisted and decided not to abort. The doctor warned that the retardation would be so severe the child would be a vegetable and would have to be institutionalized.

They had accepted such a child and then come to see me at the retreat. They asked if I would pray for the retarded child at home. I said yes I would but that I would like them to pray for the child as well in a *sustained* prayer.

"Could you pray over your child with simple childlike faith of your own for twenty minutes in the morning and twenty minutes at night?" I asked them. "Nothing noticeable will probably happen within a week or even a month—it may take a long time. It's going to take a tremendous faith on your part, but God will hear your prayer." They agreed. It took a great deal of heroism for them to do it, and God must have truly loved them for that.

The couple embarked on their daily prayer vigil. When their daughter was 8 1/2 years old, the faithful prayers had worked a miracle. What had been called an uneducable child was in a regular school in the appropriate grade with just a slightly below average IQ, receiving B's and C's in most subjects—to all indications a normal child, through faith, perserverance and prayer.

What is the prayer of faith? Does getting an answer depend upon how much faith I can muster? If I pray and get no recognizable answer, does that mean I have no faith or perhaps not enough faith? If I do pray and some great miracle happens, does that indicate I have great faith?

Sometimes persons who have lost their faith receive miraculous answers. Sometimes it is the faith of the healer, or the faith of the healed, and sometimes neither. Jesus healed the paralytic when he was let down through the roof because He admired the faith of the man's friends who went to all the trouble of removing the tiles from the roof and lowering him down into the midst of a crowd because they could not get in the door. Jesus responded to their faith to heal the man.

The woman who lost her house was bitter, her faith was

weak. She had practically lost her faith in God because of that, and yet God answered her prayer. There is a paradox here. How much must one believe in order to get the right answer? In general we can follow this principle of Jesus: "According to your faith be it done unto you."

You say you are afraid you don't have enough faith and fail to pray, and consequently lose out? So many people come within an inch of a miracle and don't get it. They do not have enough stick-to-itiveness.

It was after midnight after a healing service. I was tired but 300 people remained and the pastor asked if I would anoint them with oil. I agreed and the first person down the aisle to the communion rail to be anointed was a lady with severe arthritis. She had to hobble forward an inch at a time on crutches, a cripple for years. In my weariness I wondered why God could not have allowed the first one down to have something less severe, like a headache or a cold. But I anointed her and prayed and moved onto the next person.

A layman in the healing ministry attending the line of candidates for healing did not move along with me as he would normally do. He stayed right with the arthritic lady because he felt she was on the verge of a miracle. When I was five or six people down the line, I heard people jumping and dancing around back at the beginning of the line. There was this formerly crippled woman shouting joyously about her healing and hopping about without her crutches!

I did not complete that healing. I don't know if I did any part of it. The layman kept the vigil. He saw what I did not— that here was a woman on the brink of a healing. He was attuned to God. His faith was alive. He prayed to know whether to stay and pray or continue to move along with me. He asked the Lord with expectant faith and received his answer.

How often do we come to within an inch of a miracle because we are not attuned to what God wants, or we do not sustain that prayer long enough? Does God act because of my accomplishment in building up enough faith? Is faith automatic miracle-working power or is it something that I have to work up? Faith is not some magic power that does wonders. Jesus does the wonders, contingent on our dependence upon Him. That which brings results is a living relationship with a person— Jesus. Faith is a relationship of belief, *dependent upon the accomplishments of the One trusted*, not on the accomplishments of the one trusting.

We as exercisers of faith are simply maintaining that relationship of trust. The faith and confidence you have in your doctor is developed and strengthened by *his* success, not by yours. It is by his wisdom, his medical skill, not by anything *you* do. Your faith in him is a direct result of his accomplishments. He can help you, however, only to the degree you are willing and have faith enough in his accomplishments—the accumulation of evidence testifying to his skill—and then to follow his directions, to submit to his treatment. The analogy, I'm sure, is clear.

## Intelligent Commitment

Faith is not a prerequisite to fellowship with God, it is a byproduct of fellowship with God. The more you are united with the Lord, the greater your faith, just as the more you are in love with your spouse, the greater your trust in your spouse. So in the prayer of faith, we trust in the Person, not the prayer. I told a woman who had cancer that she did not have to believe God would heal her, only that He loved her and would be with her and do what is best for her under all circumstances. She needed to believe in His love as a *healing* love.

She felt relief. "You mean it isn't necessary for me to believe that He will heal me?"

"No," I answered, "just leave that with Him. But believe His healing love is saturating you, and then trust Him."

The woman, with just weeks to live by all medical predictions, lived five more pain-free years. She eventually died of cancer but enjoyed quite an extention of her life beyond all human expectations.

The prayer of faith is a prayer of intelligent commitment to God. It's a prayer that shares our heart's desires with God in perfect confidence. This means that if there is actually that confidence and trust, then there is no anxiety. Paul's advice from Philippians 4:7 is too often ignored. "Don't worry about anything. Instead, pray about everything. Tell God your needs and don't forget to thank him for his answers. Present your needs to the Lord."

The consequent peace that passes all understanding is not peace of mind; it's peace of soul and heart (John 14:27 and 16:33). "My peace I give you not as the world gives you..." It is the peace that operates without anxiety and is far more effective. It is an outcropping of a faith-filled trust referred to in Proverbs 3:6: "Trust the Lord completely. Don't ever trust yourself. In everything you do, put God first and he will direct you and crown your efforts with success."

Faith is dead, it's dumb, it's blind and it's ignorant. It is dead to doubts, dumb to discouragement, blind to impossibilities and is ignorant of everything but success. Yes, it's replete with paradoxes. But its optimism is irrepressible. Faith lifts up its hands through the threatening clouds and lays hold of the generous heart of Him who has all power in heaven and on earth (Acts 14:16). Faith makes the uplook good, the outlook favorable and the future glorious.

In II Corinthians 13:5, Paul says to test yourself to see if you have faith. I've presented here some tests of faith. You might try using these tests periodically to see what kind of faith you posses and to what extent. If you have especially yielding faith that believes in God's personal love for you, you will find it much easier to open yourself to God's healing love. And His compassion for you in your problems will appear more obvious.

At one Life in the Spirit Seminar, we were preparing people to receive the Baptism in the Spirit. One couple there absolutely hated one another. Their divorce lawyers had lined up the machinery for legally rupturing their marriage. Strangely enough, both had decided to attend the seminar in the midst of dismantling their marriage.

Because our team had heard about their hatred and antagonism for each other, we were secretly praying for them. Then we prayed for them to receive the Baptism in the Spirit. All that hatred and resentment that had been accumulating for years suddenly dissolved. They fell madly in love with each other and started a second honeymoon—which utterly frustrated their divorce lawyers. This was an instantaneous healing of their minds. They had been contaminated with the forces of evil. We prayed for their deliverance from the spirits of divorce, resentment and hatred before we prayed for their Baptism in the Spirit, and deliverance came. What a fantastic testimony they gave the following week, standing arm-in-arm at the microphone, telling of their miracle of grace!

The couple had not even known we were praying for them. The power of the faith of the core group worked on their behalf, even without their knowledge! Such situations show us that we have control over heaven's floodgate of power and grace. If we exercise the prayer of faith, we can do marvelous things, not only in our own lives, but in the lives of others. "In addition to all, taking up the shield of faith with which you will be able to extinguish all the flaming missiles of the evil one" (Ephesians 6:16).

The concern of a faith-filled person reflects higher priorities and is very altruistic. The faith champion often asks, "What can I do for this community, how can I enrich others, how can I contribute to community spirit, how can

I glorify God— *not merely, how can I get cured?* Hence this admonition is appropriate: Beware of a selfish attitude in prayer. A weak, almost useless faith is found in persons frequently asking to be prayed over for healing, but who seldom pray for the needs of others except their own family. These persons usually give far more emphasis to petition prayer than to praise prayer. Theirs is a kindergarten faith.

# Survival of the Spiritually Fittest

When the end time persecution comes, and it is perhaps not too far away, there is going to be a flaking off of the charismatic renewal. Only those who have deep faith will survive what's coming. There will be real hardship, mass confusion. Clergy and hierarchy may be contradicting one another, conflicting doctrines will be presented contrary to official and biblical teaching; so that many will flounder in confusion, wondering what to do, what to believe. Survival will be to the spiritually fittest—those deeply rooted in faith. Prayer meetings of hundreds will be perhaps decimated to a handful of five or six. These will barely survive, with the odds stacked against them. From these little pockets of truly faithful people, the New Jerusalem, the new church, will be built. The others will fall by the wayside.

Those with weak faith will not survive. Jesus asked the rhetorical question, "When the Son of man comes again (the Second Coming of Christ), will there be faith left on earth?" (Luke 18:8).

We see people now who have some moderate degree of faith, who play around in the lower levels of faith but who are not really cultivating their faith. They exercise faith merely to get their pains relieved. They don't cultivate faith for yielding to God's love, or faith for converting whole countries from communism, or faith to save starving millions. They cannot think of faith beyond its use to relieve an earache or a toothache; that's the tragic limit of their faith. When the pressure is really on, they will drift away. Only those will survive spiritually who have cultivated a close companionship with Jesus and absolute security in Him, who never question His will for them. Sadly, they will be few. Jesus is going to rebuild His body, His Church, with only the very best building materials available—the "remnant" few, as Isaiah calls them.

When you see a handful of charismatics in every city going around raising the dead and walking through hospitals emptying them of patients by instant healing, you will witness a spread of Christianity as never before. From the faith of these faithful few will spring forth faith throngs of other faithful ones. And God's Church will flourish as never before!

Take China with a fourth of the world's population, most of whom have never even heard the name of Christ or seen a Bible. Far less than one percent of the people are Christian. Walk into a country like that and try to evangelize it without the Holy Spirit's power, without faith-spawned miracles, and you'll find yourself butting your head against the Great Wall of China. But go in there and start curing incurable diseases by the thousands and other faith-released miracles, and watch those Chinese come flocking to Christ. In other countries, you would see countless Muslims and Jews turn to Christ. That is going to be the day, but it is going to start with a very few *faithful* Christians.

Jesus began His Church with twelve apostles. A good number of His disciples doubted Him when He started to preach about the Eucharist: "Some of you don't believe me" (John 6:64); so they left Him (verse 66). Jesus watched this winnowing process. Thousands came to enjoy His miracles and healing but at the end, how many were there at the foot of the cross? How many of the thousands of people whom He fed with the multiplied food came to

Pentecost? Only 120 followers, 120 Christians! The winnowing during Jesus' first coming will be seen again before His second coming (I Timothy 4:1).

During all the "fireworks", the "pyrotechnics" of setting up the Kingdom, everyone wanted to get in on the act, to be part of the crowd being healed or witnessing healings by Jesus, or eating the multiplied loaves, but very few had a driving desire to give consistent glory to God and followed Jesus with dedication (Luke 22:28). Those who did superficially on Palm Sunday, abandoned Him to His crucifixion five days later. That same pattern emerges again and again today. People flock to prayer meetings and charismatic Masses and retreats, but when their faith grows weak, they drift away.

God's power becomes more and more dynamic in that little handful who remain, and His future Church will explode outward from them. That is why faith is so important. That faith is lodged only in those who lovingly and closely follow Jesus, believing and trusting in His love.

This is my challenge to you. What do you want to do with your life? Do you want merely to be a Sunday morning Christian, or a builder of the Kingdom? In this age, you have an opportunity that the Church has never seen in its entire history to usher in the King of Kings.

For those who have faith, life is beautiful. For some people, each morning is "ho-hum, another day, another dollar." For people of deep faith, each morning means a new day of challenge and discovery, another day to love the Lord, "believing in His love for us" (I John 4:16).

How about you? Do you get up with an exuberant "Good morning, Lord!", or disgruntled "Good Lord, it's morning!"?

Faith, you'll find, makes all the difference.

# Taking a Second Look at the Prayer of Faith

**Ask Yourself (Or discuss with a study group)...**

1. What does it mean to believe in spite of appearances?

2. Ought we to look for a sign as confirmation of our faith?

3. What part do feelings play in faith?

4. In what ways must faith be effortless?

5. When must faith come through an anointing?

6. When must we yield to God's will in matters of faith?

7. What characterizes those who "come within an inch" of a miracle?

8. What is the essence of the peace that passes all understanding?

9. How do believers control power from heaven?

10. What crucial role does faith play in the days just prior to the Lord's Second Coming?

As a follow-up study of various dimensions of faith, it is suggested that the reader listen to some or all of the following cassette tapes by the author (other tape titles also are listed in his free tape catalog available upon request).

"Faith—Key to the Heart of God" (4-tape album upon which this book is based)

"Power in Prayer" (4 tapes)

"Getting Close to God" (2 tapes)

"Healing of Memories—Short Form" (2 tapes)

"Healing of Memories—Long Form" (6 tapes)

"How to Cope" (2 tapes)

"Coping with Worry" (2 tapes)

"The Art of Suffering" (2 tapes)

"God's-Eye View of Suffering" (2 tapes)

"Achieving Inner Peace" (4 tapes)

"Measuring Your Growth in Christ" (single tape)

Ordering information:

Single tape (approx. 1 1/2 hours): $5

2-tape albums (approx. 3 hours): $10

4-tape albums (approx. 6 hours): $18

6-tape albums (approx. 9 hours): $28

Please enclose payment with order (U.S. funds only), adding 10% for postage and handling. California residents, add 6 1/2% tax. 30-day replacement warranty for defective tapes. Prices subject to change.

Order tapes and books from:

CLARETIAN TAPE MINISTRY
P.O. Box 19100
Los Angeles CA 90019
Phone: (213) 734-1234

# PEOPLE OF THE WAY

By Edith J. Agnew

*Illustrated by Johannes Troyer*

THE WESTMINSTER PRESS

PHILADELPHIA

*Think about these words—and learn them:* Matthew 28:19–20; John 13:35; Acts 4:20.

"Within Our Quiet Church, O God," by Jean Lillie Hill. From *Hymns for Primary Worship*. Copyright, 1946, by The Westminster Press.
"A Grace," attributed to Mary Rumsey.

Scripture quotations are from the Revised Standard Version of The Holy Bible, copyrighted 1946 and 1952 by the Division of Christian Education of the National Council of Churches, and are used by permission.

Library of Congress Catalog Card No. 60–5618

PRINTED IN THE UNITED STATES OF AMERICA

## JESUS MAKES A PROMISE

Peter and Andrew, James and John, and the other disciples were standing on a hill not far from the city of Jerusalem. Jesus was there too, talking with them as he had done many times during the last three years. But this time was different.

A few weeks before, they had seen Jesus killed, and they had not expected ever to see him alive again. But then an amazing thing happened. On the third day, Jesus had risen from the dead. He had been coming and going among them ever since. Now, he said, he must leave them, and they were listening to his words as they had never listened before.

"Stay in Jerusalem," Jesus was saying, "and wait for God's power to be given you. Then you shall speak for me, first in Jerusalem, then in all Judea, then in Samaria, and then in all the world. Go therefore and make disciples of all nations, baptizing them and teaching them to observe all that I have commanded you; and lo, I am with you always."

No one else spoke after that. No one could. In the stillness that followed Jesus' words, a white cloud rolled over the hilltop. When the cloud was gone, the disciples could not see Jesus any more. But

they were sure he would always be with them in some way. He had promised.

Peter started down the hill with great strides. He had always been big and strong. His work as a fisherman on the Sea of Galilee had hardened his muscles, and lately he had become used to walking mile after mile with Jesus.

On the way down to the valley below another disciple asked, "Peter, what shall we do now?"

"We must go back to Jerusalem and wait—as Jesus told us."

"What do you think will happen?" the disciple asked.

Peter did not know the answer. "We'll wait and see," he said.

The other disciples could hardly believe what they heard. Peter had never before been willing to wait for anything!

All the way to Jerusalem, Peter kept remembering his life with Jesus. He remembered when Jesus had found him with his brother Andrew washing nets beside the Sea of Galilee and had said to them, "Come, follow me." They had been with the Master ever since.

Sometimes Jesus had been pleased with Peter, and sometimes he had been disappointed. When Jesus asked a question, Peter was likely to blurt out the first thing that came into his head, before he had time to think. But even when he made mistakes, Jesus had always forgiven him.

I don't understand Jesus, Peter thought.    I don't understand half the things he told us or half the things he did.    I don't understand why he had to die, or how God raised him from the dead.    I don't understand what is going to happen now.    I only know we must obey the Master.

By this time the disciples had reached the gates of the city.

Several of them were saying, "Where shall we go now?"

One group decided: "We'll meet in the upper room of the house where we have been staying, coming there quietly one at a time.    We'll ask Mary to join us, and Jesus' brothers, and those we can trust."

And so they gathered in that upper room, waiting and wondering, praying together that God would make them able to do whatever he had for them to do.

8

# THE END OF WAITING

Something strange was about to happen. Those in the upper room hardly knew what to expect, but they felt that Jesus' promise would soon come true. God's power, Jesus had said, would come to them if they waited and prayed. And they had waited and prayed for many days.

Peter and John were there, and the other disciples who had been closest to Jesus. Jesus' brothers were there, and his mother, and a number of other women. About a hundred and twenty had gathered, as they had been doing each day.

Today the streets below were full of excitement, for Pentecost had come, the festival at the end of the grain harvest. The Jewish law said that all Jewish men, wherever they lived, must appear at the Temple in Jerusalem during this season.  And so the city was crowded with people from Galilee and Samaria, Egypt and Arabia, Greece and Rome, parts of Asia, and islands of the sea.  In other years the disciples would have been in the streets too, mingling with friends and strangers. But not this year.  They must keep on praying.

In the street outside the house two men stopped to listen.

"What is going on up there?"  one asked the other, motioning with his thumb to the high window.  The other shrugged his shoulders.

"Who knows?" he answered. "Nothing good, you may be sure.  I see people stealing in and out of that house every day, looking as if they had a great secret."

"They are probably plotting against the government," said the first man.   "Perhaps we should report them."

"Not yet," replied the second.   "The city is full of reports already. No one would pay any attention to us.   Let us wait until the feast is over."

"Yes," agreed the other, "but let us keep our eyes and ears open. Something may happen."

They moved on down the narrow street.   They could not even imagine what really was happening in that upper room.

The disciples had greeted one another.   They had asked about those who were sick or in trouble.   They had spoken of Jesus' last days with them and reminded themselves how often they had failed him.

12

Perhaps they were failing him now. They ought to tell his story to the people who had come to the feast, but they were not sure how to make themselves understood.

"He expected us to speak for him," said one, "but we are not able."

"We are still afraid," said one of the women.

"Let us pray to be forgiven," said another.

"And pray that God will teach our tongues to speak," said still another.

The prayers were begun.   One person did not wait for another to finish.   Many were praying at once, some speaking aloud.   They praised God for his goodness.   They thanked him that they had known Jesus and that they knew he was alive.   They asked for forgiveness. They prayed that they might know what to do next and have the strength to do it.

Just then there came the sound as of a rushing mighty wind, filling all the room, and there appeared to be flaming light touching every person.   Suddenly no one was weak or afraid any longer.   Everyone felt strong and full of courage.

The gift of God's power and strength and wisdom had been given, and the people in the upper room cried out with joy.

# NEW DISCIPLES

When Peter and the others who had been praying in the upper room came downstairs, they were like different people.   They wanted to sing. They wanted to shout.   They mixed with the crowds, talking to strangers from many lands, telling the story of Jesus to any who would listen.

Peter heard somebody say in surprise: "Listen to these men from Galilee!   They have never had much schooling.   How can they speak

as they do?'' Peter did not answer, for now there was something more important to say.

Hundreds of people had gathered, wanting to know what all the excitement was about. Some belonged in Jerusalem and nearby parts of Palestine. They remembered the days when Jesus had come to this same place to teach beside the pillars of the porch. They remembered what had happened to Jesus. Some of them had loved him and wanted

17

to follow him; some of them had hated him and wanted him to be killed. But others had come from far-off places and did not know much about Jesus. Many of them had never even heard his name.

Peter pushed his way up the steps through the curious people at the doorway and looked down on the crowds below. Now was his chance to speak as Jesus had commanded, he thought. Did he dare? Did he dare speak out, not only to friends but to strangers and enemies? Yes, of course he dared!

He lifted up his hands to quiet the crowd, and his voice rang out.

"Jesus of Nazareth," his words sounded clearly, "the one you put to death, is the one God promised to our people long ago. We know, because God has raised him from the dead. With our own eyes we have

18

seen him and have spoken with him, and he with us."

As Peter went on, more and more people gathered to listen. Some were not much interested in what he was saying. They just wanted to be wherever there was excitement.

Others whispered to one another: "This speaker may be dangerous. He reminds people about Jesus, and we would rather forget him. We must keep an eye on this man."

Still others listened eagerly, pressing closer and closer to Peter.

"These words are true," they said to themselves. "Jesus is indeed the one God has promised all through the years. We were wicked to let him be killed. We have done wrong in many ways. What shall we do?"

They crowded around Peter and said: "We believe what you have said. We are ashamed of ourselves. Tell us what we must do."

"Turn from your wrongdoing," Peter told them. "Be baptized in the name of Jesus, and come join us."

That day about three thousand men, women, and children were baptized and joined those who met with the disciples to learn more of Jesus' words and acts.

20

Together they listened to the teachings of the apostles, as the first disciples were called.   Together they prayed and worked.   They came to be known as the people of the "Way"—Jesus' way.

# THE PEOPLE OF THE WAY

The people of the Way did more than talk. Since Jesus spent so much of his time helping those in trouble, they wanted to help others too. They visited the sick, the poor, the anxious and lonely, and shared what they had with those who were in need.

But their enemies were looking for excuses to find fault with them, and sometimes even acts of loving-kindness got them into trouble.

One afternoon Peter was going to the Temple for the hour of prayer. John, another of the apostles, was with him. Peter and John had been friends ever since the days when they had gone fishing together on the Sea of Galilee.

As the two men came near the entrance called the Beautiful Gate, they noticed a lame man sitting there, holding out his hands.   He was calling to those who went by: "I have been lame all my life.   Give, please give!"

"I have no silver and gold," Peter said, "but I give you what I have. In the name of Jesus of Nazareth, stand up and walk."

The lame man grasped Peter's hand and was pulled up on his feet. He found he could stand, he could walk, he could even run! He went into the Temple with Peter and John, walking and leaping and praising God.

All the people who saw the lame man walking were filled with wonder and crowded around Peter and John in great amazement.

Peter said to them, "Why do you marvel at us, as if we had made this man well by ourselves?" And he spoke to them of Jesus, whom they had killed, but who was alive again.

"It is only in his name," Peter said, "that this lame man could be made strong." And he asked the people to turn from their wrongdoing and believe that Jesus was the one God had promised to send to them.

When the priests and the ruler of the Temple saw the crowd and heard what was being said, they arrested Peter and John and sent them to prison for the night.

The next day the priests held a trial, and again Peter spoke boldly. All who listened were surprised. What had happened to Peter and John to make them such powerful speakers? And how could they heal a man

who had never walked?   That man was standing in the room with them, so they could say nothing against his story.   They sent Peter and John out of the room while they tried to decide what to do with them.

"We cannot say their story is not true," they said, "but we must keep it from spreading any farther.   Let us tell Peter and John that they must speak to no one else in Jesus' name again."

Peter and John came in.   "We command you," said the high priest, "not to speak or teach at all in the name of Jesus."

But Peter and John replied: "Do you think we should obey you rather than God?   We cannot help speaking of the things we have seen and heard."

Finally they were allowed to go free, for the priests were afraid to punish them any more.   They went back to the other disciples and explained what had happened.   Then they all praised God and prayed that they might go on speaking about Jesus with courage.

From this time on, the people of the Way began to live apart from others in Jerusalem.   They shared with one another everything they had, because they remembered Jesus' commandment, "Love one another as I have loved you."   Those who had lands and houses sold them and brought the money to the apostles, who used it to care for the hungry and homeless people among them.   They did all this with joy, even though they knew that being different from the people around them would get them into trouble.

# BEYOND JERUSALEM

The people of the Way could not go to the synagogues or to the Temple any more, for the priests had forbidden them to worship there. They had to find other places to meet, often in one another's homes. And as they gathered together week after week, they began to be called a "church."

One evening during such a meeting, the mother of the household said to her daughter, "My child, make sure that the outside gate is fastened securely and that the door is locked."

While the girl ran to obey, her mother hung a dark cloth over the window so that the lamplight could not be seen from the street. People in the room were speaking in low tones. Even the smallest children seemed to understand that no noise must be heard outside. The man called Paul, who hated them, might try to break up the meeting.

After a while the meeting began. Instead of reading from the scrolls, the neighbors reminded one another of Jesus' words and acts among them. Then one of the men began to pray. In the middle of the prayer came a dreaded sound. Knock, knock! Knock, knock!

Three men were pounding at the outer gate. Without waiting for an answer, they broke the latch, entered the yard, strode up to the door of the house, and pushed it open.

"Who is the head of this house?" demanded the first one.

The prayer went on. "Whatever happens, O God of our fathers, give us strength and courage. Keep us mindful that our Master has promised to be with us always. In his name. Amen."

One of the group rose and faced the three men. "I am head of this house," he said. "What is your errand?"

"We have orders to arrest you," said the second man.

"Who gave you the orders?"

"The chief priests," answered the third man, "and Paul."

30

"Paul!"   As the name was whispered around the room, the children hid behind their mothers' skirts.   The very sound of that name frightened them.

The three men led the owner of the house off to prison. By twos and threes, the others at the meeting went to their own homes, dreading what Paul might do the next day.

A few days later, the man who had been arrested and had been released from prison after a severe beating, went to see Peter. "We cannot stay here in Jerusalem," he said. "It is not safe for the children. Our family and some others have decided to leave the city. We will go as soon as we can sell our houses and pack the few things we can carry."

"I am sorry this must be," Peter said, "but I believe you are doing God's will. Where do you plan to go?"

"To a city far to the north," he answered. "Perhaps to Antioch or Damascus."

32

"God be with you," said Peter, "and help you to speak for the Master wherever you go."

During the next few weeks the apostles said good-by to other families. Although it was hard to lose so many from the church in Jerusalem, they saw that what Jesus had told them was beginning to happen.    Now men, women, and children would speak for him in places beyond Jerusalem.

# "BROTHER PAUL"

The families that had to move from Jerusalem to Antioch and Damascus went to the synagogues there and were not driven out. Yet they would often gather in one another's homes for friendly talk and meals and

worship.    It seemed good for the people of the Way to be together.

Then one day frightening news reached Damascus: "Paul is here in the city."    Paul, their greatest enemy!

Fathers and mothers looked at each other with trouble in their eyes.

"Will we have to move again?" one of the women asked her husband.

"Perhaps—we do not know.    God will show us what to do," was the answer.    But even the children could see that their mothers and fathers were worried.

Days went by.    Every day the people of the Way expected the dreaded knock at the door.    Every day they expected Paul to begin arresting people and sending them to prison.    Yet the city was very quiet.    What could have happened to Paul?

Then one evening the people of the Way were invited to the home of Ananias, who was a leader among them in Damascus.

When one family coming through the doorway saw who stood beside Ananias, they almost drew back. The man was Paul! As the father and mother stood still for a minute, they saw that Ananias had his hand on Paul's shoulder and seemed not at all afraid. They went on into the room, just as Ananias began to speak.

"We need not fear Paul any longer," Ananias said. "Hear what God has done for him.

"He was on his way from Jerusalem to Damascus, with letters from the high priest giving him permission to seize our people and take them prisoners to Jerusalem.

"Paul had made up his mind that not one of us should escape.

"But along the way a blazing light blinded him and a voice spoke to him. It was the Lord Jesus.

"When Paul reached Damascus, he was still blind. The Lord told me to go to him; but knowing how much evil he had done, I was afraid. Then the Lord said to me: 'Go, for I have chosen Paul to carry my words far and wide. I will show him how much he must suffer for my sake.'

"So I did as the Lord said. I found Paul praying. When I laid my hands on him, he could again see. He has been baptized and has become one of us. *You must believe this.* He too is a follower of the Way."

The people in the room asked themselves, "How can we believe?" And then they looked at Paul. His face showed no hatred, only love and joy. They said to themselves, "We have heard the truth."

One by one they came near to Paul, took his hands, and called him "Brother Paul."

When the Jewish leaders heard of this, they were angry and tried to find and punish Paul. But his new friends helped him to escape. They knew that God had work for him to do.

# INTO ALL THE WORLD

As time went on, Peter and the other apostles in Jerusalem began to hear news of those who had left them. Some of this news was hard to believe, for it was about Paul, their old enemy—now said to be preaching and teaching in "the church in Damascus." But soon they knew that what they heard was true, for Paul had come to speak in Jesus' name even in Jerusalem.

The apostles heard from "the church in Antioch" too. Those who had moved there asked for a teacher because so many Greeks were joining with them. James and Peter decided to send Barnabas to Antioch, for he understood and spoke the Greek language very well.

Barnabas found much to do in Antioch, and since he needed more help, he went to Tarsus for Paul. The church grew as Paul and Barnabas worked together. And the Greeks in Antioch gave a new name to the people of the Way. They called them "Christians."

One day while a few Christians were worshiping together, God made them understand that he wanted them to do something that had never been done before. One of the men spoke what was in all their minds.

"The story of Jesus has been told beyond Jerusalem and beyond

Samaria.  The church is growing here and in Damascus.  Has the
time now come to send the message farther?"

"Yes!" said all who had gathered.  "But whom shall we send?
Who will go for us?"

They decided that God wanted them to send Paul and Barnabas, their own best teachers.

And so Paul and Barnabas made ready for a long journey. Before they left Antioch, the church people prayed with them, asking God to keep them safe on their travels and make plain to them what they should say.

Wherever Paul and Barnabas stopped they had adventures. In one city they met a magician who tried to have them arrested. In another, they healed a lame man, and the people called them gods and wanted to worship them. Often they were put in prison. In one place Paul was stoned and almost killed.

    At the end of their journey, Paul and Barnabas came back to Antioch, and then went on to Jerusalem, stopping at many places in Phoenicia and Samaria.   Wherever they went, the people of the church gathered to hear what God had done through them as they preached and taught. Paul reported, "In all the countries we have visited, Greeks as well as Jews are believing in the Lord Jesus."   And the listeners heard the news with joy.

45

Some of the Christians in Jerusalem could not understand how Greeks and others who were not Jews could become disciples. But as the leaders in the church talked together of all that the Lord Jesus had said and done, they became more and more certain that he wanted everyone who believes in him to be a part of his church.

47

They had never forgotten the words Jesus had spoken on that hilltop just before he left them:

"Then you shall speak for me, first in Jerusalem, and then in all Judea, then in Samaria, and then in all the world. Go therefore and make disciples of all nations."

The apostles themselves had not been able to go into all the world, but others were beginning to do so. Someday there would be people of the Way in all nations. They would know that the words Jesus had spoken were true. He would be with them always.